Making Space

Also by Jayne Hardy

The Self-Care Project
365 Days of Self-Care: A Journal

Making Space

Creating boundaries in an
ever-encroaching world

Jayne Hardy

First published in Great Britain in 2019 by Orion Spring
an imprint of The Orion Publishing Group Ltd
Carmelite House, 50 Victoria Embankment
London EC4Y 0DZ

An Hachette UK Company

10 9 8 7 6 5 4 3 2 1

Illustrations by Dominic Hardy

A CIP catalogue record for this book is
available from the British Library.

ISBN (Trade Paperback) 978 1 4091 8345 7
ISBN (eBook) 978 1 4091 8346 4

Every effort has been made to ensure that the information in the
book is accurate. The information in this book may not be applicable
in each individual case so it is advised that professional medical
advice is obtained for specific health matters and before changing any
medication or dosage. Neither the publisher nor author accepts any legal
responsibility for any personal injury or other damage or loss arising
from the use of the information in this book. In addition if you are
concerned about your diet or exercise regime and wish to change
them, you should consult a health practitioner first.

Typeset by Goldust Design
Printed in Italy

MIX
Paper from
responsible sources
FSC® C104740
www.fsc.org

www.orionbooks.co.uk

Contents

Dedicated to Dommy, and Peggy

Introduction

It's a dog eat dog world out there, and if we don't make and hold space, we're jostled and elbowed from every which way; physically, mentally, emotionally, culturally and spiritually.

Everything we do, say, think, allow and tolerate is connected to boundaries. Our routines, habits, choices and relationships. Everything. These boundaries are the 'start', 'stop', 'here I am', 'not on your nelly' and 'no entry' road-sign equivalent to our lives. When our lives naturally intertwine with others, there will be limits to what we deem acceptable and not acceptable. These limits illustrate who we are, how we'll conduct ourselves, the divvying up of responsibility, and attest to how we wish to be treated. We all have these limits which flex depending on the nature of the relationship: familial, paternal, romantic, friendship, working, and the one we have with ourselves. Sometimes these limits become wonky, compromised and violated, and ultimately work not for us, but against us.

Along the way, we've collected a considerable back catalogue of boundary baggage which determines how empowered or disempowered we feel in asserting them. Every telling-off, slamming of our bedroom door, hug, choice of outfit, diary entry, compromise, decision, standing up or standing down, is a boundary-shuffle in action. The consequences of those – whether they were respected or disrespected; whether we respected or disrespected – will factor into how we feel about boundaries now. Whether we realise they even exist; how wonky, assertive, confident, connected, isolated, seen, heard or walked on we might feel.

Ideally, we'd all be conscious and comprehending of who we indeed are, what makes us tick, and feel able to communicate that clearly and effectively. But the opposite is quite often the case. Perhaps we're not entirely sure about who we are, of what makes us tick nor how to communicate our needs with others. Maybe we've never quite felt as though we measured up. Perhaps we've always felt as though we're in the way, that we don't matter. That feeling of insignificance then permeates how we view ourselves and all that surrounds us. It dominates the jobs we apply for, or don't apply for. Our yeses and our nos. Our relationships, how we parent, what we apologise for, how we hold ourselves, whether we're an active participant in this thing called life or whether that perception of insignificance keeps us stuck, accepting our lot, rather than relishing in it.

Make no bones about it, learning about boundaries and what they mean for us is the easier bit because that's on us. It's the holding steadfast in them when it comes to other people and external circumstances that can cause a bit of a ruckus, some friction, and plenty of deep breaths as we have the courage of our convictions. We're all worthy of boundaries which keep us safe, happy and healthy. It's learning how to cohabit with others in a safe, comfortable and healthy way, where boundaries are vulnerable to going off-piste. We want others to be happy and might forgo our happiness for that to happen. It's not our role in life to sidestep, duck, move out of the way to make life easier for others. It's truly not. We're allowed to take up space too. We're allowed to feel joyous, heard, seen, significant, equal, lit up by life and as though we matter.

And so, here we are, about to dive headfirst into a book about boundaries. A book which explores our understanding of what boundaries are, how they can be applied to different situations, finding our feet and our voices, and unpicking some unhelpful lessons we've learned along the way. You can start by asserting your boundaries in how you read and use this book; perhaps you'll read from cover to cover and return to the worksheets after that. You might dive into the chapters which speak loudly to you as areas of your life which you feel have boundary deficits. And you might tackle the worksheets, in the first instance, to help figure out what's causing the most amount of life-chafing for you right now. There might be writing in margins, highlighting, screenshotting and talking to others about what crops up. Your book, your way.

Jayne x
PS. You can find me online – come and say 'hi!':
Twitter   Instagram @jaynehardy_

1. Who am I to write this book?

Learning about the concept of boundaries was like opening a window into a parallel world: a world where I felt more in control, calmer and not so trodden on. A place where I had a say, was heard and was not afraid to challenge the status quo. Somewhere I could sense my backbone, stood tall, felt better and wasn't scared to take up space. Albeit a place that made me panic slightly at what all of that meant for someone who had lived their life, thus far, people-pleasing – how on earth did I get from where I was, to there?

That window into a parallel magical healthy-boundary world came from a really tough period in my life, and it would take considerable time before I felt brave enough and centred enough in myself to start constructing boundaries that served my health and happiness without feeling incredibly selfish for doing so.

Boundaries are a funny ol' thing, they can keep us safe, they can keep everything out, but they can also keep us in 'our place'. To challenge them often means going against a grain, a grain somebody somewhere has carved out. For as long as I can remember, I wanted to be a 'good' girl. It felt like high praise from my parents and teachers, and so I became intuitive about what that meant for me; doing as I was told, not causing 'trouble' and avoiding disappointing anyone or being told off. It also meant I tied my worth to receiving that praise that I held in such high esteem; it meant an awful lot to me that I was viewed in a certain way and I most definitely wanted to be 'liked'.

We won't ever be everyone's cup of tea, but golly, I tried. Inevitably, someone somewhere wouldn't like me, and I would replay every word, every look, every action to understand why and what I must have done wrong. The onus, in my head, was always that I was at fault, that I was to blame, that there must be something wrong with me. Notice too that I didn't give space to how I felt about others and whether I liked them or not. Anyone and their dog were welcome to take up my headspace.

I learned to become a chameleon; I identified behaviours that I could change into, like we might change an outfit for a different occasion. These behaviours meant I could adopt and adapt and align with whoever I was with. The result? I never ever really felt as though I fitted in anywhere. Being a chameleon is awkward; you never understand your baseline, preferences, or give space to your own opinions. And you're impressionable. If my peers liked a band, I'd buy the album and jolly well like the band too – even if I didn't, not really. In my quest to be all things to all others, it meant I ended up compromising myself. I lost any semblance of identity; I tried to become what others wanted and needed me to be. Talk about making a rusty rod for my back.

It wasn't half a fearful way to live. There was no room for mistakes nor for the natural messiness that occurs as we all grow and muddle our way through life. I spent an awful lot of time inside my head, dwelling on things I'd said or hadn't said. Things that had happened aeons ago would play on my mind. The overwhelming feeling was of guilt. I felt guilty for everything – even the stuff I'd had no hand in. Guilt became a baseline, and I would do anything to avoid it. I took responsibility for things I had no right/authority/need to do so. In some ways, I was giving away my power, but in other ways, I was letting myself believe I had a more influential role in other people's lives than I could/ should ever have. It was an apologetic paradox. 'Sorry' became my most-used word. You bumped into me? I'm so sorry I was in your way. I've said something you don't like? I'm really sorry, I didn't mean it in quite the way it came out. I've done something you don't approve of? I'm ever so sorry, I won't do that again. I need the loo. Sorry to be a pain and to make you drive out of your way to find a bathroom for me. Sorry, I just need to... Sorry, sorry, sorry, sorry.

It all came to a head in my early twenties, and 'sorry' became a more sinister 'sorry I exist'. It seems that bending over backwards and tying yourself in knots to keep others happy and taking responsibility for things and people that are absolutely not your responsibility is a highway to hell – saying 'yes' when you keenly mean 'no' breeds anger and resentment. The floodgates to that anger would snap open when I'd go out drinking with my friends. Add social anxiety to the mix and I'd smash all personality-based boundaries loose by drinking far too much so that I felt more comfortable being out and about, but in doing so, I became an angry, belligerent and hurtful drunk with hangovers

'Saying "yes" when you keenly mean "no" breeds anger and resentment.'

that would make me cringe as I remembered the things I may have said or done. Talk about adding fuel to that well-established inward-looking and apologetic nature of mine. I started loathing myself, and on top of the over-apologising, regrets were growing on top of my regrets. I was in a pickle as I was also working a job I didn't enjoy – another example of my lack of boundaries.

You're pressed to make decisions on what you would like to do with your life at secondary school, and I didn't have a clue what that might look like. When I was little, I'd wanted to be a vet until I realised that being a vet involved operations and things, it wasn't just cuddling with cute animals. After that, it seemed as though being a teacher might be all right, but that meant university, and I had a boyfriend at that crucial 'applying to university' time who was opposed to me swanning off to a different city. Being so malleable meant that my teaching plans were knocked on the head and past that, I truly didn't have a clue what I'd like to do or be. In that pre-internet age, I didn't realise the extent of what was possible either – our careers advice was based on going to university for going to university's sake, or joining the armed forces. In true wonky-boundary-style, I ended up referring the somewhat life-altering decision to my tutor. I mean, I stayed true to my patterns of behaviour, even then, and then some. I asked him what I should do, and he replied that being accomplished at mathematics, I might want to try accountancy. And so, I did.

Alas, it wasn't for me (you knew that was coming, didn't you?!). Worse still, I didn't know what *was* for me. I left that job and trotted off to university, but even then, my lack of boundaries got in the way; I would go out most nights even when I didn't want to because it was what everyone was doing, and I would overdrink and overspend. I was just going with the flow of everyone around me. Missing structure, not being very interested in my course, feeling unanchored, I started to feel my mental health decline. I went home one Easter holiday and only returned to university to collect my things.

Reflecting on all of this (and more), compassionately, is hard. There is no rewind button nor flux capacitor, and I feel sad that I continued to give away my power at every which way. Whilst there was a smile on my face, a willingness to please and a mask that hid any unease I felt, I grew more and more disjointed and disenchanted with life. I felt as though I was swaying this way, that way, forwards and backwards and still, I couldn't do enough nor be enough. I didn't know who I was nor what I wanted but kept getting swept away by other people's wants and dreams and passions. It all got a bit wonky and stressful. It wasn't long until depression reared its ugly head and knocked me for six.

Landing at rock bottom with a resounding thud was torturous, and I felt a deep sense of shame. Apathy meant that I didn't care enough to put on the smiley mask and I retreated from everyone. Being alone was more comfortable than being surrounded by the people I was trying to keep happy, placate or please. Being alone, though, was pretty awful as I'd grown to dislike myself intensely. Not liking yourself is uncomfortable as there's no breather from oneself; it's a 24/7 experience with no let-up. Depression is a cruel illness as, in essence, your very being is at war with itself. Your body which works so efficiently to keep you alive comes up against a brain that feeds you a barrage of negative, disempowering and frightful thoughts. The loss of hope and isolation make it an unstable, uncertain and scary place to be. I was there for an extended period of time and have been back a fair few times since. In that pitch-blackness, my boundaries swung the other way, like a pendulum. Extremely rickety and fluid ones were replaced with walls of stone and gates of steel whereby I didn't let anyone in. The people-pleasing came to a sudden halt, but I was also keeping the good stuff at bay. Those dark times – that I still fear to this day – have been the undoing of me and (though I hate to give them any credit) the redoing of me.

Managing my mental health has been a long learning curve/ crawl. A process of tweaking, pivoting and flexing. It's mostly trial and error as I navigate new things to see if they'll help, or not help. Boundaries and self-care go hand in hand. Without boundaries, we might understand the importance of self-care but not protect the space within which to do it. Whilst self-care became the foundation where my actions of self-kindness slowly became louder than my negative self-talk, boundaries became the framework I built to protect my physical, mental, emotional and digital space. I wish I could say it's been easy, but that annoying adage is true – nothing worth having seems to come easily.

Creating boundaries when we've not had many, to begin with, changes relationships – often for the better as balance is redressed, but sometimes relationships don't stand the test of healthier, more equal boundaries. Once the power is distributed more equitably, some relationships sadly don't survive. Boundaries sort the wheat from the chaff but what we're left with is precious and honest and sincere. This boundary-work comes with growing pains too, as we strive to undo old habits and create new uncharted ones. Speaking up and out, honestly, takes courage we can't always muster and some getting used to, and not forgetting the boundaries of others and how we navigate the marrying of those with ours.

Nowadays, my boundary pendulum hovers somewhere in the middle; still needing work at times, still swinging ever so slightly to people-pleasing as new experiences like motherhood or leading a team take time, require conscious thought, boundary-creating, communication and learning, but they've eventually gotten to a healthier place. I've finally arrived at a better place too with a stronger sense of identity, dreams, opinions, moral compass and possibilities.

In a small nutshell, that's where I've been, where I am and why I'm writing this book. As with most things we focus on, what we zoom in on expands and we see it everywhere. That's what this boundary malarkey is like; I find myself talking, learning and thinking about it a lot. Anyone who knows me now can attest that I'm always willing to talk about this stuff. They're super important because they underpin our relationships with everyone and everything. It's not a concept that has passed others by, either. Yes, there's uncertainty about what the nuts and bolts of boundaries are and indeed, about how to put some of this into place, but people are coming to realise that there are habits they have that are starting to annoy or restrict them. If I can positively use my somewhat tricky experiences to help you feel more powerful, assertive and confident, then that is what I'll try to do here, in this book.

Eleven times my boundaries have left a lot to be desired

Gah, boundaries. If only I knew then, what I know now. It would have saved me a ton of heartache, heartbreak, uncertainty and that awful sense that you have the word 'mug' tattooed on to your forehead.

For me, boundaries were an odd concept because as a child you look to your parents and your teachers to learn from them. Not once are we told that we could question those people; we're urged to 'respect our elders', to 'do as we're told' and I definitely would have felt that to come up against them would have been disrespectful. We don't get an inkling, either, that our parents are winging life and learning as they go; they seem so together and so sure of what it is they're doing and saying.

As a child, I did all of the things I thought I was meant to do: I listened, I did as I was told and for the most part, I was a 'good' girl. There were exceptions, of course! Like the time I ran away to my auntie's house which was just behind our house, or when I wrote on the newly painted pristine-white door and blamed it on my sister who couldn't yet walk, let alone write. My mum has this look, and we call it the 'Walters glare' because all of her siblings have the same expression. It's a look that you don't want to be on the receiving end of, and it pretty much says, 'Are you sure that's what you want to do or say? Consider this is your chance to stop whatever it is, right this minute.' Dad's equivalent was a wagging finger, and it was equally as powerful. I recall hating the words 'I'm disappointed in you'; they felt worse than any proper telling-off and still to this day, I have a fear of disappointing people or bearing the brunt of their anger.

Once adulthood arrived, it all came a bit undone. Having spent the preceding years planning all of the adventures I'd have once I got to the grand old age of eighteen when I could 'do whatever I wanted', it turned out I wasn't quite prepared for that freedom. Creating, and holding, boundaries when you've never done so is unsettling. It's like taking the baton in a relay race you never signed up to nor trained for.

And so I drifted and became unhappier and unfulfilled. I tied myself in knots because in looking to others to guide me on what I should do, to tell me what I should do, I ended up trying to keep everyone else happy. It didn't go particularly well, as you can imagine, and perhaps attest to. With that in mind, I'm about to share the very tip of my wonky-boundary iceberg, with you.

1 YES, OF COURSE

You could have asked me to do most things, and my kneejerk reaction would be to say 'Yes, of course'. With an emphasis on the 'of course' so that the asker would be reassured that this was 100 per cent no problem, exactly what I wanted to do and that I would help. The trouble is, that a good chunk of the time, my automatic 'Yes, of course' was an 'Oh no, why have you asked me, how do I say no to this?!' Cue merry dances as I would try to come up with plausible excuses to backtrack. I'd wince as I cancelled plans at the very last minute. I'd feel so worried that I'd done that enough times that I appeared flaky. I'd be buoyed by guilt and end up having to see whatever it was through. Not only was I making a rod for my back, but it also muddied the waters of communication. My 'Yes, of course' started to be met with 'Are you sure?' because of all the prior cancelling and backtracking, and instead of being honest, I'd even more emphatically declare 'Absolutely, yes'. In wanting to be 'good old Jayne, she'll do anything for anyone' as though that's something to be applauded, I learned that 'doing anything for anyone' is absolutely not a byline to aspire to.

2 THERE ARE STARVING CHILDREN IN THE WORLD

I think all children of a certain generation were fed this line. It was commonly used when you didn't eat all of the food you'd been served up, and parents wanted to see an empty plate and for us to be grateful that there was food on the table. And whilst I can understand the importance of children being brought up with an awareness of their privilege, I don't think to eat for eating's sake teaches that lesson all that well. As a child, I ate more than I needed to beacause it was important to 'eat it all up'. When I speak to my parents now, it's clear that they inherited that old chestnut and were using a blueprint afforded to them – that they hadn't questioned. To this day, I still clear my plate. Even when I don't like the food, even when I'm full up and even when I have been served a ridiculously large portion. Scraping my leftovers into a bin continues to be a source of guilt. Rationally, I understand there are much more constructive things I can do, and do do, to help those in need, but some boundaries are more ingrained than others.

3 KNIGHT IN SHINING ARMOUR

When things went downhill for me and depression hit, I would hope and hope and hope for someone to come along and fix my life, and my brain, and me. As if, by magic, they'd telepathically sense my pain, my wishes and my all-at-sea-ness and ride in on a white stallion and sprinkle fairy dust and take over and everything would be just fine and dandy. There's a part of now-Jayne that admires the sheer fairy-tale-ness of then-Jayne's mind. But there's a sadness on reflection too, that I had learned such helplessness and spent so long riding out those tough days, waiting and wishing to feel better. Compounded also by the boundaries I tended to construct around myself that prevented me from asking for help in the first place. In wishing with all of my might that someone else would swoop in and help unstick my life, I was underestimating myself and overestimating what other people could do – particularly considering this was a time when I wasn't even helping myself. I remember when someone on Twitter told me, not in the kindest of ways, that my wishbone was where my backbone should be, and it stung. It stung hard. But it was true, too; I was hoping that someone else could help me in ways that I could help myself. I could be my own knight in shining armour.

4 OPEN HOUSE

Both my husband and I are introverts, and our home feels like a sanctuary where we can restore, wear our scruffiest comfies and recharge. As much as I'd like to be the sort of person whose home is open for people to rock up whenever they fancy, there's nothing quite like the thought, or reality, of people turning up unannounced to set off a bout of panic. It doesn't matter who it is or how much we love them dearly; it feels like an infringement on our privacy. Working from home makes it trickier too; people assume that you can drop everything for a prolonged cuppa when it suits them with no consideration for whether it suits you. The inner conflict that arises from this is that we're unreasonable and rude in wanting some advance notice, because when I was younger we'd show up unannounced to our relatives' houses and they didn't mind. Or did they? That is the question!

5 ENDLESS MEETINGS

Oh boy, I've come full circle on meetings and very rarely have them nowadays when a Zoom or a conference call will do. Old boundary-less-me attended every meeting I was asked to participate in – my diary would be jam-packed with meeting after meeting after meeting. It was a minefield because you'd have to allow a buffer for travel and a buffer in case the meeting overran. A considerable amount of time was spent either rushing to the next meeting in earnest or twiddling my thumbs because I'd built in too generous a buffer. I've probably lost months to meetings, and travelling to meetings, that neither bore fruit nor moved any plans further forward. I've attended meetings where I've been bored witless and left not really grasping what the meeting was even about. The good meetings were always few and far between. Some people love meetings and have meetings about meetings, but I'm definitely not one of them.

Living in Cornwall and working with people who reside in London is always a funny one for me, too. There's still an assumption that I'll pop to London for an hour-long meeting at the drop of a hat. In reality, it takes four hours of travel, both ways, for that one-hour meeting – that's a significant time cost without factoring in the monetary cost and the parental sacrifice that comes with not being there to do my usual parenting stuff, which I love being around to do. And, that's on a good day, when the meeting falls smack-bang in the middle of the day, and I can get there and back on the same day. We're not even factoring in train delays here. Nowadays, my diary is relatively meeting-free. It feels liberating: I'm more productive, less knackered, and yet I still get to work with incredible people and organisations who are London-based.

6 BRUSHING THINGS UNDER THE CARPET

When addressing a problem with someone or when a situation arises where I need to assert myself, I still get sweaty palms, a racing heart and an overwhelming urge to run away and hide or procrastinate, or worst of all, fall in line. I now know how to overcome those nerves and tend to address situations head on, and it works out better for all involved, and I welcome it the other way too. Old me? Oh dear. I'd preferably have sawn my arm off with my teeth than have to assert myself and/or confront someone. It means that I've accepted some pretty unacceptable behaviour in the past, I've put up and shut up for way longer than has been healthy to do so and I've buried the anger, resentment and self-esteem-battering that comes with doing that. It seems that brushing things under the carpet doesn't make them go away; it merely stocks up the 'things I need to address' into an overbearing and painful pile until it topples you and leaves you with your self-esteem in tatters.

7 RECOVERY TIME

At the age of twenty, I had my four wisdom teeth removed under a general anaesthetic and, as advised by the hospital, I booked a week's sick leave from my job at an accountancy firm. The operation went without a hitch, but the stitched holes in my mouth were painful, and the anaesthetic knocked me for six. When I returned to work, I was called into the office of one of the partners, who wanted to discuss my recent absence. I explained that I'd had an operation to have my wisdom teeth removed and he told me that taking a week of sick leave was unacceptable as, and I quote, he 'had returned to work the same day after having his removed'. As someone who has recently booked a week off work for another upcoming operation, I understand that the unacceptable-ness in this situation wasn't coming from me but from his expectations that I should be like him and return to work, regardless of the fact you're not allowed to drive the same day you have a general anaesthetic, anyway. But this reprimand left its mark for a long time – it told me that work was more important than my health and I believed it, to my detriment. It taught me that I had to turn up to work as quickly as possible, no matter the circumstances, and without it affecting my performance in any way. It showed me that business could be cold and uncompromising. That's the trouble with always respecting your elders and accepting everything that they say; you can sometimes end up adopting unhealthy and damaging beliefs.

8 HAIR DISASTERS

I used to be the person who would smile at the hairdresser as they would hover the mirror behind your head to show off your new 'do' and then promptly burst into tears once I was safely outside, out of view. For some reason, my brown hair takes on any warm tones in dye, and it goes orange. Not auburn, orange. I've had a Geri Halliwell do when I've been seeking a Gisele vibe, even when I'd patiently explained the warm tones thing. There have been orange all-overs which I've tried to rectify at home, ending up with a patchy, stripy mess. I'd never speak up; I'd pay, and I'd even leave a tip for the privilege of hating my hair.

9 TRUSTING MYSELF

My gut sometimes barks at me, and I've learned to trust what it's telling me. I've come to understand that our bodies have all kinds of clever ways to communicate with us what's right for us and what needs attention. We're intuitive and instinctive. On reflection, there have been some humdingers of circumstances which would absolutely have been avoided had I not gone against my better judgement, and if only I'd trusted my gut. From senses about people, to whether I'm being sold a tale or two. Times I've quietened my doubts and compromised myself because I've placed a higher value on other people's expectations, wants and needs.

10 ARE YOU SITTING COMFORTABLY?
Because I'm not sitting comfortably. Well, actually, I am *right* now, but if we head back to March 2014 when I'd just given birth to our daughter, there's an incident that stands out as being particularly rife with dodgy boundaries and no, I was most certainly not sitting comfortably.

Nothing really prepared me for the physical aftermath of giving birth; the aches, the pains, the tears, the fatigue, the milk-laden boobs and the sheer excruciating pain of having stitches in your undercarriage. Oh my, ouch, ouch and then plenty more ouch multiplied by a hundred quadrillion million ouches.

As is so common, everyone you love descends for those precious newborn cuddles, and I honestly didn't mind. It felt like a miracle that we had our daughter and that she was healthy (after a scary birth story that I'll save for another day). We didn't mind sharing the love at all. But at the time, we lived in a flat that you wouldn't have been able to swing a cat in. Seating was a sofa or the floor. People would come and see us, and I'd end up sitting on the floor; that was the norm. So, yes, mere days post-birth, I ended up perched on the hard floor, stitches an' all. As. Was. The. Norm. Nobody offered me a seat on my sofa despite the perhaps somewhat passive-aggressive overdramatised wincing and 'ow'-ing. It never occurred to me that I could just ask for a more comfortable place to sit.

11 WONKY-TONKING

There's this pervasive sense that people don't like me, that I'm simply not likeable. Rationally, I know that what other people think of me is none of my business but still, it feels sketchy. The real question I should be asking is what is it about myself that I consider to be so darned dislikeable? Which leads me down the garden path to understanding that perhaps, sometimes, I don't like myself much at all. I'm tying in what other people 'might' think of me – based on no substantial evidence too – with how I feel about myself. And that there, is a merged, wonky-tonk boundary and a half.

Times my boundaries have left a lot to be desired	What it taught me

Who, or what, is encroaching on your space right now?

Date	The 'sorrys'

Keep track of all the unnecessary 'sorrys'

2. What are boundaries and why are they so difficult?

Boundaries are inescapable: they're the physical, mental, digital, emotional, environmental, spiritual and cultural constructs that create a framework which underpins and influences how we behave, our expectations on how those around us might behave, what we take responsibility for, what others take responsibility for, what we let in and what we keep out, and the relationship we have with ourselves and everything around us.

Everything we do, feel or see has a boundary linked to it in some way – even if they're not always so glaringly obvious. There are the clearly defined, mostly man-made boundaries that we can see everywhere we look: the fences, the walls, the hedges, the bridges, the borders, the gates. The homes we live in have doors, walls and windows which determine the boundaries of our residence. Those doors and gates and windows and walls and hedges set limits on who can go where, and when, and how. These physical boundaries can help us to feel safe and protected and they act as limits and guides for others. They're clear, easily communicated and asserted, and flexible – we can lock a door and unlock a door depending on the circumstances. We can invite people in, and we can shut people out.

If our homes are ever broken into or something happens to compromise these physical boundaries, we might start to feel unsafe in our homes and up the ante on our security. We might build a wall topped with barbed wire, install security alarms, sensors or stronger locks. Anything to decrease the risk of an infringement of those boundaries, and the inherent danger. Fortifying these boundaries might give us a sense of security but they also make it more difficult for the people we love and like to get in. And that's something we have to bear in mind with all of our boundaries; that they're not so fortress-y, so inflexible, so rigid, that they prevent the good from getting in.

How we've been brought up, the values and cultural habits which are instilled and influenced by our caregivers will affect our boundaries. How we communicate and the language we use, how we conduct our interpersonal relationships, how we deal with conflict, how we view power and authority, the foods we eat and when we eat them, the clothes we wear day-to-day or for occasions, how we respect ourselves,

'That's why this boundary stuff is so important; we're a generation that's out of sync – being swayed this way and that way by societal pressure, societal shoulds and societal shifts.'

whether we hug, shake hands, nod, wave or kiss two cheeks as a greeting, whether we have a fixed or growth mindset, the pace and space we apply to areas of our lives such as our attitude to work or family time. These help make up the boundaries we have with ourselves; a sort of blueprint or internal guidebook that we each hold inside. It contains all sorts of inherited, adopted and learned information about who we are and what we'd like to do, about where we begin and where we end. A code of self-conduct which includes our likes, our dislikes, our beliefs, our needs, our values and our identity. When we align our boundaries with our values, we create an environment within which we can thrive.

It stands to reason that the opposite must also make sense; when we're feeling off-kilter, disconnected, overwhelmed, overcommitted, disrespected and frazzled, as though life is a soap opera with unrelenting drama, there's a boundary there somewhere that's misaligned with our values and in need of some negotiation and management. That's why this boundary stuff is so important; we're a generation that's out of sync – being swayed this way and that way by societal pressure, societal shoulds and societal shifts.

According to a study carried out by the Mental Health Foundation, in 2018, 74 per cent felt so stressed that they have been overwhelmed or unable to cope.[1]

---

1 Source: https://www.mentalhealth.org.uk/publications/stress-are-we-coping

The Co-op and British Red Cross carried out a study about loneliness which revealed that over 9 million people in the UK are either always or often lonely.[2]

The World Health Organization estimates that there are more than 300 million people in the world living with depression right now.[3]

Data from the survey, 'Mental Health of Children and Young People in England, 2017', reveals a slight increase over time in the prevalence of mental disorder in 5 to 15-year-olds (the age group covered on all surveys in this series). Rising from 9.7 per cent in 1999 and 10.1 per cent in 2004, to 11.2 per cent in 2017.[4]

What Does a Healthy Boundary Look Like?

Boundaries can be cast in iron and uncompromising; they can be looser and easily compromised; they can be non-existent and symptomatic of a low sense of self. They set the tone for what we will, and will not, tolerate.

Healthy boundaries are clear, not too constricting or overpowering of others, designed by us, adaptable to differing

---

2 Source: https://www.redcross.org.uk/-/media/documents/about-us/research-publications/health-social-care-and-support/co-op-trapped-in-a-bubble-report.pdf?la=en&hash=32EDC253C12C3466CD39267417507E467A44CA2F
3 Source: https://www.who.int/mental_health/management/depression/en/
4 Source: https://digital.nhs.uk/data-and-information/publications/statistical/mental-health-of-children-and-young-people-in-england

situations and people as we see fit, not damaging to us, nor to anyone else. They force us to consider our limits and to respect the limits of others, as well as ensuring we take responsibility for our happiness and allow others to do the same. They communicate when we've had enough or have given all that we are prepared to give.

When our sense of identity is a strong, self-assured, self-confident one, it's clearer to us (and to others) how we wish to go about our days and ways; we won't drink a drink if we don't like it, we won't date people we don't feel connected to, we value our time, our energy, our health and our values, and have no qualms protecting them.

Low self-worth makes this boundary stuff all the trickier. If we tie our self-value in with how happy we make others, how productive we can be, how useful we can be, how many life creases we can iron out easily for others, if we avoid causing any ripples, at all costs – even when our boundaries are compromised – we're going to end up all wonky-tonk and out of sync with ourselves.

When Boundaries Go Wonky

Misaligned and wonky boundaries are interesting because we all have oscillating limits depending on who, where and what we're dealing with. Our tolerance levels are interchangeable, boundaries fluid. But there will be some boundaries which are absolute, ones we hold steadfast – there will be things we just can't see ourselves ever doing, no matter what, since to do so would contradict and contravene our core selves, our morals and principles.

There are some behaviours, too, which are always completely unacceptable, whatever the circumstances – when our feelings are brushed off and invalidated, when people tell us how we think and feel, when we're physically touched in inappropriate, painful or unwanted ways, when others use fear to get us to co-operate, when their opinions are forced upon us; having to parent our parents from a ridiculously young age; parents who instil their beliefs in to us and don't allow us to question them; and when issues are repeatedly brushed under the carpet.

Infringed-upon, compromised or non-existent boundaries can feel like: being manipulated or controlled, excluded or lonely, unsafe, frustrated, angry, backed into a corner, disrespected, stuck, being a puppet on a string, having no autonomy, being overextended, confused, scared of upsetting someone when we speak up, trodden on, full of resentment, shouldering undue blame, disconnected, trapped, powerless and beholden to assumptions placed upon us.

Just as the land borders and boundaries around us are ones we readily accept as pertaining to a continent, a country, a town, a home, we must be aware and mindful of the other boundaries we may be readily accepting that don't serve us. The ones we've learned from our parents, our teachers, from society and from those in power.

Boundaries don't count for much though, unless we communicate them clearly, are willing to assert them when we feel they have been violated and are prepared to uphold the consequences that come into play when our boundaries have been breached despite our assertions.

This stuff is far from easy or simple, and here are some of the reasons why:

We're Not Always Taught this Stuff

We're not. We're taught how to tie our shoelaces, how to read and write, about history, geography, the sciences, how to bake cakes, how to take care of others and so on, but we're rarely taught how to take care of our mental and emotional health, or that it's something to be prioritised. It's an alien concept to lots of us that we can indeed say no without dire consequences and even if the consequences are undesired, that we can and will get through them. It's mindboggling to some of us that we have choices and the autonomy to set limits for ourselves and those around us. It's never occurred to some of us that feeling safe and happy is way more important than feeling nice. And we're not taught that being kind to ourselves isn't always the same as being kind to others – sometimes the balance tips too far and we become over-accommodating. If we're not made aware of this power within, we don't know it's there. If we're not given the opportunity to practise this stuff as young people, then as adults we find ourselves on wobbly waters.

Wonky Messaging

The messaging surrounding all of this can be so mixed up too, often unintentionally. Tell a child often enough to do as they're told and funnily enough, they will, and they'll keep doing so, to their detriment. We're urged not to make a fuss, and so we try our darnedest to be 'good' and not rock the boat. We tell girls that when boys are mean to them, it means they like them very much, which teaches both girls and boys that unreasonable behaviour is acceptable in some situations. When we make mistakes, like spilling our cornflakes or breaking a toy, we're admonished, teaching us that mistakes absolutely aren't okay. We're urged to apologise when we've done something or said something wrong but aren't necessarily apologised to by our parents when they've done or said something amiss. We're told always to be honest, and then we're told off if our honesty isn't of the 'right' kind. We're encouraged to respect our elders, but what about if they behave disrespectfully?

In our formative years, we're always looking to the people around us to learn from, to help us to take 'form'. If those people around us don't understand boundaries, don't align their actions with their words, don't present examples to us of their limits in a clear and consistent dialogue, then as adults, we have a great deal of unlearning and relearning to do.

We Fear Rejection

The fear of rejection is a pervasive one and can have a massive impact on our lives. It can prevent us from speaking up and speaking out, from putting ourselves forward for job roles that we're more than qualified for, negotiating contracts, it can see us turning down dates, bowing to peer pressure, self-sabotaging, getting pro at people-pleasing and basically, avoiding any situation or conversation where we might be judged, criticised or rejected.

This is all linked to low self-esteem and every time the fear wins out, we're reinforcing the story we tell ourselves about how we're unworthy, that we will only be accepted by being 'good', by masking our true feelings, or behaving how we believe people want us to be. We often feel inauthentic, as though we're going to be 'caught out', because we *are* being inauthentic; we're casting aside our true values and opinions and limits, so that we won't be cast aside, and we're fearful of showing our true-ness in case we end up alone.

This doesn't half lead to cockeyed boundaries though – we end up putting up with things waaay past the point that they became unhealthy for us. It often results in enabling bad behaviour, not taking a stand against wrongdoing against us, experiencing burn-out as we rabbit away trying to please others, living reactively and not proactively, ignoring our own needs, and as for those dreams of ours, they were kissed goodbye a long, long time ago.

We might worry that setting a boundary will end up in us being rejected in some way, but if people are scared so easily away just because we've identified and set limits for ourselves, then they're the ones who were most in need of the boundaries in the first place. Our not having boundaries has probably over-served them for far too long and they've rather liked it that way.

Boundaries Themselves Are Misused and Misunderstood

Boundaries can be misused as a means of control, coercion, manipulation or to build barricades around us. We might experience this as having overly strict parents, when our privacy is dishonoured, we're lied to or someone is sneaky behind our backs and keeping us in the dark, in encountering people with a strong sense of entitlement, a boss who dictates our every action, a partner who insists in knowing our every move or is abusive, people who act as though they respect boundaries but incessantly try to chip away at them even with habits such as food; if we overindulge, we might decide to go on a diet, whereas it's healthier to be mindful of our relationship with food every day, rather than a means to punish ourselves. It might be that we've experienced trauma and to protect ourselves, we pull up the drawbridge – keeping the 'bad' out but also, in our rigid defence, blocking the good.

Boundaries or Barricades

There's a difference between crafting boundaries and building barricades. Healthy boundaries are not insurmountable walls that are set in stone and impenetrable, just as they're not trampled on and destroyed non-existent limits. They're not the push-pull, reflex rebellion or barricades we build around us to block everything out. Boundaries are rational, come from self-awareness, allow us to encounter life at our own pace. They help us to maintain a healthy relationship between us and all else. They encompass our standards, what works for us and what doesn't. Barricades come from a 'life is black and white' place, whereas boundaries take into consideration all the multiple shades of grey. Barricades mean we're always primed to defend ourselves, to don our shield and guard which depletes our energy. Boundaries protect our energy, enabling us to function effectively. Barricades are rigid, impenetrable, block intimacy and cause isolation. Boundaries are malleable depending on circumstance. They deepen and strengthen relationships and connection. Barricades are born from a place of fear and can hold us prisoner. Boundaries are born from a place of hope and provide freedom.

Sometimes We Learn the Hard Way

There are infinite boundary scenarios we will go through and grow through, as we evolve and change, as will our limits and needs. We'll have different sets of boundaries in divergent areas of our lives and for our varying relationships.

Foresight is the perception we bring to bear on any given upcoming chain of events. It's the ability to predict what might happen based on a back catalogue of knowledge and experiences. It can be really useful in understanding that if it's going to rain then we might want to equip ourselves with a coat, an umbrella and appropriate footwear.

What it's not great for is helping us to predict things we've never experienced or have no knowledge of. That's why our romantic relationships can be a minefield and so angst-ridden during our teenage years. Having never navigated boundaries within a romantic relationship, we're going to experience the push and pull and compromise and uncertainty and pain which converts our foresight into hindsight for the future. If we're lucky, we'll have grown up seeing healthy relationships around us which serve as boundary templates and give us the chance to borrow other people's foresight, but if we didn't, we'll learn the hard way, and man, it hurts to wade through that.

We might beat ourselves up with self-criticism, but we quite literally don't know what we don't know. Building that back catalogue of experiences and knowledge takes time; it's trial and error, and often, we won't know we were missing a boundary until it hurts, until we experience the pain, frustration, anger, resentment, all the knee-jerk reactions and feelings we experience upon an infringement.

There's nothing about setting and holding boundaries that's comfortable. Nothing. It's a case of living through the short-term awkwardness for a longer-term gain.

We Don't Press Pause

Life is a series of micro and not-so-micro decisions that we make. Some are inconsequential but others have the ability to shift our life path and completely alter our trajectory – we won't always know the difference between the life-changing ones and the more seemingly mundane ones at the time these decisions arise. It's by glancing back through our lives that we can clearly see how the course of our lives was adjusted by a sole decision, or series of decisions, that we made.

As emotional beings, it's fair to say that choices and actions and behaviours can be emotion-led – influenced by an internal reaction to an external situation, conversation, challenge or event. When something makes our blood boil with anger, or fear makes the hairs on the back of our neck stand on end, when insecurity makes us want to push people away before they

'There are three sides to every story: yours... mine... and the truth.'

can distance themselves from us, or excitement creates that feeling of having a butterfly farm inside, we don't always press pause on that; we often feel compelled to react instantaneously, with rather emotion-clouded judgement.

At that moment, though, we're put to the test. We have choices (we always have choices): volatility or calm, a measured approach or a spontaneous one, irrational or strategic, to seek clarity or to dive in with blinkers on. Emotion derails our rationale and logic. How many times have we fired off a text message in the heat of the moment, only to regret it later? Perhaps we have a forked tongue when angry and we say things that aren't at all a true representation of our real thoughts and feelings. That time we honked our horn from frustration or lashed out because we felt jealous.

Those emotional reactions are based on what's gone before, our unique take on any given life event; it's not always as is. There's a quote by Robert Evans: 'There are three sides to every story: yours... mine... and the truth. No one is lying. Memories shared serve each differently.'[5]

Whilst there are universal truths we share, that are based on fact, when we reminisce with people, the way the memory is told might differ from how we remember it. Nobody is remembering wrongly, necessarily, the memory is simply swayed by our emotions and opinions and the story we've written for ourselves.

---

5 Robert Evans, *The Kid Stays in the Picture* (Viking, 1994)

'What we can do is create and hold space for the feelings, to allow ourselves to feel whatever it is we are feeling.'

When it comes to how we might react, their reactions stem from the same place.

What we can do is create and hold space for the feelings, to allow ourselves to feel whatever it is we are feeling. It's akin to pressing a pause button, which in turn gives our emotions room to cool down and makes way for that logical reasoning side to pop its head up. That pause is oh-so-precious because it allows us to examine the 'other sides' of the story, to exercise compassion and self-compassion, to find calm within the chaos and to communicate in a fair and considered and non-reckless way. Most of all, it allows us to make sure our decisions lead to an outcome that supports our values.

Boundaries Can Feel Like Rejection

When our boundaries are wonky-tonk and we're met with someone who has less wonky-tonk boundaries, we can feel blocked by them, uncared for and as though they're unavailable to us. This is especially true for those of us who are new to this boundary stuff. If we would bend over backwards for others, jump to their needs and do whatever we can to help them, and that's not returned, it can feel as though the non-returner is mean-spirited, uncaring and doesn't hold us in as high esteem as we hold them. It can really hurt.

That is, until we realise that their boundaries are absolutely nothing to do with us. Nothing at all. But our boundaries – they're completely our business. You see, we have to get to a place where a 'no' from someone doesn't impact on how we feel about ourselves – because it's their right as much as it's ours, to say 'no' – we can't, and shouldn't, tie our self-esteem to the actions of another. Sometimes it is our expectations that are too high, too assuming. When we give, and we do so willingly, with no agenda, that's not a 'pass the parcel' kind of furore. We must only give when we're 100 per cent willing to do so, with no obligation on the recipient to 'return the favour'. We don't give to receive; we give because we want to.

In valuing ourselves and all that we are and all that we have, we must also value the same in others. If, when limits are communicated to us, the story we tell ourselves is one of abandonment and rejection, then we might avoid asserting our boundaries, as we don't want others to feel abandoned and rejected by ours. It just opens the door to mixed messaging, passive aggression, walking on eggshells, mind games and guesswork. When we're on the receiving end of a 'no', that's not typically a rejection of who we are, it's that the person doesn't feel equipped nor wants to offer a 'yes'. The clarity and honesty are to be embraced, whatever the answer might be.

We mustn't ever try to influence the boundaries of another. Of course, the flipside is true, too; we have every right to create space in and around ourselves, and to prioritise our needs without guilt or fear of consequence. It's our individual right to create a life that's peaceful, tops us up, to say yes or no when something is asked of us.

We Don't Understand the Difference Between Assertion and Aggression

Holding space is hard. It requires us to stand firm and to be willing to follow through on consequences when our limits are disrespected. The trouble with this, for those of us who haven't had much practice in doing so, is that we can feel hostile and combative when we do it, as though we're being aggressive.

There's a chasm of a difference between assertion and aggression, in both the delivery and the receiving, yet we so often confuse the two. When we stand up for ourselves and what we believe in, we can do so respectfully, honestly, mindfully and calmly, with an open-mindedness and willingness to negotiate if need be and to acknowledge conflicting views – that's assertion. Communication is kept friendly; body language is relaxed with eye contact and we genuinely listen to hear. We don't want to 'win' to the detriment of another, we simply want to affirm our beliefs and opinions, and not compromise ourselves in the process.

Aggression is a whole different beast and it's what happens when someone exerts their rights to get the outcome they desire in an overbearing, pushy, exhausting, sarcastic, sometimes humiliating, intimidating and violent manner. Talking over others, a dedication to getting our own way, threatening, puffing out our chest to make ourselves bigger, wild gesticulating and invading someone else's mental and physical space are hallmarks of harmful aggressive behaviour.

And let's not forget about passive aggression, as it doesn't feel like either of those two – it almost feels harmless, but it's detrimental nonetheless, and perhaps more common. If, throughout our lives, standing up for ourselves and expressing our needs was frowned upon, discouraged or even inhibited, then we might find it a proper struggle to do those things. When we opt out of standing up for ourselves and expressing our needs, we might find ourselves engaging in passive-aggressive behaviour as a way to express our upset – indirectly expressing hostility by sulking, procrastinating, that shrill 'I'm fine' when we're anything but, withdrawing emotionally or giving the silent treatment, burning the toast on purpose, deliberately not 'liking' someone's posts on social media to convey annoyance, the sub-tweeting, 'accidentally on purpose' ignoring someone as we pass them in the street, dishing out subtle insults, avoiding or belittling someone we're upset with, or being overly critical. What's so interesting about passive aggression is that we use it to avoid confrontation, but it nearly always results in confrontation or the dissolution of a relationship, because it can create mental or emotional harm, as well as ambiguity.

If we consider which of those we'd rather be on the receiving end of, assertion probably ranks highest for us all because it's also the clearest and kindest. Something to bear in mind when we consider how we communicate our boundaries with others. Being assertive does *not* equal being aggressive, but it can 'feel' aggressive if it's passive aggression we're used to.

When have you felt that pang of rejection
as boundaries are shuffled?

What are you putting up with?

Stockpile some 'assertive' responses

- _____

- _____

- _____

- _____

- _____

- _____

- _____

3. Making space for who we are and what we need

It's okay to have boundaries. It's more than okay to build support systems, safety nets, space around and inside of ourselves. It's sensible, practical and does wonders for our health, happiness, relationships and self-confidence to have emotional, mental and physical limits. But oddly, it can quite often feel far from okay.

We mightn't realise it, but we all hold a vision of who we are and of who we'd like to be, to grow into. It starts when we're younger, with the 'When I'm eighteen, I'm going to [insert exciting plans here]'. They don't always pan out how we'd envisaged, but we tend to have a plan, a timeframe, in our mind's eye where we can see ourselves doing certain things by a certain time. Of course, life isn't lived that way, and the plans go awry, get curtailed and sometimes, we change our minds; but this vision

'The boundaries we create protect our identity and make room for all that's important to us.'

makes up part of our self-identity, and that's the basis for a lot of this personal boundary work: that we know who we are and understand that as a person, we're independent of others. The boundaries we create protect our identity and make room for all that's important to us.

There's stuff we instinctually know to be true for ourselves which forms the building blocks for our identity and underpins how we relate to the world around us. For example, if we've tried Marmite, we'll know whether we love it or hate it. We might have a favourite colour, a favourite smell, a list of favourite and not-so-favourite foods, and there might be a place we've been to where we felt oh-so at peace. There will be certain things that make us laugh and certain things that make us cry. We might identify as an introvert, an extrovert or an ambivert. At school, we may have adored PE but abhorred science. There will be people we're drawn to and those we have an inexplicable not-so-nice reaction to in our gut. There will be social causes which we find more emotive than others. Horror films might scare us witless, and rom-coms might be our bag. The opposite of all of the above may be true for you. We're the beholders of a wealth of conscious and subconscious information which only we're privy to; a library of all of our needs, wants, dreams, wishes, ambitions, likes and dislikes, visceral reactions and personality traits. Only we will know when a person, situation or circumstance conjures up an inward groan or butterflies of excitement, a heavy heart or a skip in our step, that awkward feeling or a sense of pure comfort.

It's the holding true to ourselves and honouring who we are, and who we want to be, that can get a little tricky when you add other people into the mix. As a social species we yearn for a sense of belonging, of connection and intimacy with others – according to Maslow's Hierarchy of Needs, these are our psychological needs. As well as a need for all of that,

'An indicator that our boundaries need some work is when our belonging needs feel at odds with our esteem needs.'

we also have esteem needs; a need to feel self-respect and be respected by others, to feel a sense of achievement, that we're good at things, to have recognition and self-esteem. An indicator that our boundaries need some work is when our belonging needs feel at odds with our esteem needs, or that neither are being met.

Authenticity has become one of those words that's bandied about in marketing campaigns galore and along the way it's lost its meaning, its core. When we don't assert who we are nor honour who we are, we lose our meaning too. The essence of who we are becomes lost as we bend, mesh, toe the line and be who we think we need to be for other people. And we feel that lack of truthfulness with every inch of our being – it's tiresome to keep arranging ourselves to be more agreeable for others. We end up not saying what we mean nor meaning what we say. We iron out the kinks and quirks to pave the way for a quieter day, to make life easier and okay for every Tom, Dick and Harry, Brenda, Philippa and Barry.

Whose Choice Are We Making?

Every day is rife with choices and decisions; according to some sources, we make a whopping 35,000 conscious decisions per

'When something isn't given freely, it's stolen, or we feel held to ransom, and that's no way to live.'

day! Some of those decisions we'll avoid making, others we'll deliberate over and over. There'll be those we'll make impulsively, and some where we'll make the decision to people-please and comply with what feels to be the popular option. These ongoing decision-making processes compound one another. Aristotle said: 'We are what we repeatedly do. Excellence, then, is not an act, but a habit.' When we repeatedly compromise ourselves, we'll end up with the essence of who we are being compromised. This reasoning applies to everything we consistently do over and over and over again; people-pleasing, squishing ourselves to fit into societal 'norms', falling into patterns of expected behaviour, hesitating before we challenge something, saying 'yes' when we mean 'no'.

In the toss-up between compromising ourselves and compromising with others, we might take what feels like the more straightforward, less fraught, route; we do what we can to make life easier for others, despite the ramifications or cost that might yield for us and the personal boundaries we might be flexing. When we flex (or demolish) our boundaries, it doesn't necessarily come with a lightning bolt of warning and raising of our hackles; it can feel good and generous and kind and less turbulent than to rock the boat. In isolation, this doesn't always feel like such a big deal, and it isn't always. It's the persistent flexing when our instincts whisper that we should assert that upsets the apple cart. When we hold steady in quietening and dampening our inner compass and end up doing things which feel uncomfortable, laden with resentment and inauthentic, it's damaging to our self-esteem and self-confidence. It teeters too, the distribution of power – we hand over our power on a platter. In being what we deem to be selfless, we often become self-less; our identities merge with those around us until we feel as though we're a hodgepodge of a person. And nobody wants that for somebody they care about.

Whilst it feels kinder to acquiesce to those we love and care about, it's unkind to them, and us, to not hold space for who we are. When something isn't given freely, it's stolen, or we feel held to ransom, and that's no way to live. There will be repercussions, and there's no doubt about that. We can't keep giving what we don't have to provide or want to offer; we all have limits, and at some point, the bough will break when it's under too much pressure. That's what happens to us when we keep flexing, pivoting, tweaking and bowing to someone else's tune. We stumble, we run out of steam and we end up angry, resentful and buckled.

Headspace

It's not selfish to de-wonkify or make space for ourselves. It's imperative. Once those boundaries are in place, it's kinder to communicate them clearly and honestly than to swat them away. Boundaries help us to make room for all that's important to us in our lives – not what's important to other people, but what we have consciously appraised to be important to us. Our role in life isn't to conspire with others to pave the way for their

'It's not selfish to de-wonkify or make space for ourselves. It's imperative.'

needs and to make their lives rip-roaringly easy, all the while needing more and wanting more and deserving more. For as much as we may love, adore and care for others and support them in honouring themselves, this relationship malarkey is a two-way street.

On an intellectual level, we can understand something to be valid and rational and sensical. We can understand the importance of boundaries, want to do something about them, understand our 'why' and yet we don't feel quite sure as to how to go about it all. As complex beings, there's a three-way tug-of-war that occurs between our biological make-up and what we want to do and what we do. There are layers upon layers of psychological and biological and emotional wiring that we're up against. We can think of these as our baseline behaviours, the 'norm', the habitual natures we revert to when we're tired, decisioned-out and under pressure.

There will be things about our baseline behaviours that irk us or that we wrangle with when trying to set limits or create boundaries for ourselves. Whether it's that we tend to people-please, be fearful, overeat, overspend, binge drink, under-sleep, are self-conscious, easily distracted, fall into scroll-holes or have a resistance to routine, for example. These are all boundary issues.

Where there's a tendency, sometimes, to take responsibility for too much, the opposite can be true. Dishing out daily blame willy-nilly without ever considering how our actions may have contributed to a situation or consequence is another way of relinquishing all responsibility and personal power to others.

Some of the hardest boundaries to identify and establish are those boundaries we have with ourselves. We might have a grasp on who we are, who we'd like to be, what we'd like to do, and a list of things we wish we either did or didn't do. It feels simple enough, doesn't it? In identifying the behaviours we'd like to change, we ought to be able to, you know, replace them. Right?

Unfortunately, it's seldom that easy because everything we do is underpinned by a need that's fulfilled by our current (learned) behaviours.

We might be able to identify which behaviours we need to change and feel as though it's as simple as setting out with good intentions, and we feel buoyed up, confident and motivated. When we flounder (as is likely when we're trying to change our behaviours because it's challenging to do) we don't chalk it up to learning, we become furious with ourselves, and the positivity and motivation ebb away. If we try again, we do so with the recent stumble hanging over our heads. Our confidence gets knocked, and because we are wired in such a way that we're oversensitive to the perceived negative and under-sensitive to the perceived positive, it's harder the second and third and fourth time around – once bitten twice shy.

Where to begin?

With Enough-ness and Establishing Limits

You are enough. Even when you don't feel it, you are enough. You are enough, particularly when you feel as though you are lacking, falling short, jaded, unworthy, too this and too that, frazzled, dropping   *'You are enough.'*

balls, making mistakes, not yoga-ing, or when your floordrobe and adulting gets too much – you are still enough. It's a universal truth that we are all enough as we are, in the right here and now.

Don't waste time, energy and heartache on comparing where you are with where other people 'appear' to be. Appearances are deceptive and those shiny, smiley, edited pictures you see across social media never tell the full story. Not ever. They never could. We're complex things, us humans, and we have the capacity to smile in the bleakest of times. A photo shows what we want it to show. Our captions share what we feel comfortable in sharing.

In the same vein, don't waste time, energy and heartache on being who you think everybody else wants you to be – they don't get a say over that, at all. You get carte blanche to be whoever you want to be. The only approval that matters is that you approve of you. Live truthfully and honestly according to that. Be kind to yourself about those mistakes, they're a sign you're trying different things, and that's a positive thing.

Not feeling we are enough can mean that we don't feel equal to our peers. When it comes to this boundary thing, it matters because we're less likely to feel able to assert a boundary and stand up for ourselves if we feel we don't measure up. Our natural negative bias means that we're always going to feel as though it's a fight to change, because it is – we're fighting the habits our brain loves so dearly; our mind wants what's easy and uses less cognitive fuel. Change can feel negative, even if we know it's needed. The negative will feel magnified too because we're wired for that to happen,

'Don't waste time, energy and heartache on being who you think everybody else wants you to be.'

but we can stockpile letters, screenshots, emails, photographs, anything that we receive or mementoes of what we've done that counteract that negative bias somewhat.

You are enough. No ifs, no buts

When it comes to establishing the limits of our boundaries, we'll all be aware of a time when we felt manipulated. An instance when we were spoken to in a way that set our hackles rising, when someone has encroached on our personal space, emotions have been used to make us feel guilty, or when we feel someone has overstepped the mark in making fun of us. Whilst horrible things to experience, we can turn those experiences into limits – we know what we find unacceptable and intolerable. Next up, it's the application of that reasoning, and consideration, to all of our boundaries: physical, emotional, digital, mental, spiritual, work and verbal. Some of these boundaries will be flexible – we might feel comfortable in trusting a friend with something confidential and not feel the same way towards another person. We might love to hug a loved one but not want to let another into that physical space. Other boundaries will be non-negotiable; there are things we will never accept nor do, and these vary from person to person.

Limit Stress

We've all got this nifty fear-o-meter which scans our horizons for threats. In days gone by, this feature was incredibly useful

'Limiting stress is a boundary issue.' and kept us safe from danger. This inbuilt facility has no off switch, nor has the fight or flight instinct quite gotten to grips with our current technology-rich cultures. In theory, it's designed to keep us safe from threats, but it is overly sensitive, always on, and errs on the side of caution rather than take a risk by ignoring something that could later be harmful to us because once upon a time that could have been the difference between life and death. A hormone called cortisol floods our bloodstream whenever a threat is detected, so that we're poised to react. That's typically good stress; if we need to be stronger, run faster, respond quicker, then cortisol is the hero of the hour.

And then there's the not-so-good side of stress. The side that, according to the World Health Organization, is an epidemic of the twenty-first century.[6] You see, cortisol has its place against grizzly bears and woolly mammoths but in our current climes, not so much. The continual drip-feed of cortisol is a contributing factor to: memory loss, decreased cognitive function, increasing anxiety, decreased libido, inhibited immune system, increased size of our amygdala which is the fear part of our brains, increased risk of high blood pressure, obesity, diabetes, depression, heart disease, stroke and heart attack.

The more we feel stressed, the more the regular bits and bobs of our everyday lives start to feel scary, and the more primed we are for action. In reality, we're frazzled, close to the end of our tethers, overwhelmed, put-upon and as though we're racing through life

---

6 Source: https://www.researchgate.net/publication/312003144_Stress_ Concepts_Definition_and_History

at high-speed dub. We adapt to this pace of life without realising the short-term and long-term implications of that. Non-stop stress wears us down and wears us out.

Limiting stress is a boundary issue. It's about creating space and protective measures so that there's ample chance to top up energy levels. It's about shared responsibility, delegation, mindfully considering the demands on our time, changing our minds and choosing wisely. It's in how things feel to us; those inward groans, the stomach drops, the knots of anxiety and using those feelings to help us make choices which support our health and happiness, rather than working against them. It's accepting that we're not limitless and that, like all living and mechanical things, we need to be maintained, serviced and given a break.

Prioritise Sleep

Sleep is king, and that's no understatement. When we're unsure of where to begin with boundaries, we can look at the things which might be preventing us from having a good night's kip and create a framework around that to support us getting the sleep we so need and deserve. When we're rested and refreshed, everything else feels so much more do-able.

When we're tired, everything feels like too much trouble, even the easy stuff. If we're endeavouring to create and consistently assert the boundaries that matter to us, we need all the rest we can get. Sleep helps us to keep motivated, stay focused, retain clarity and on track with our new habits. It's one of the reasons we put off starting things until Monday comes; there's

'Not only is our sleep a boundary that we can assert and protect, being rested will help us to have the energy to assert boundaries in other areas of our lives.'

the assumption that we'll feel refreshed and raring to go, after a rested weekend.

Our lives are non-stop *go, go, go* from the moment we wake up to the moment we get into bed. And even then, we're slicing and dicing considerable blocks of time from the section of our day that's set aside for highly valuable shuteye. We're burning the candle at both ends. We're also expecting to be able to just fall asleep at the drop of a hat whilst simultaneously doing so much during the day that will affect how likely that it is to happen.

Sleep deprivation causes havoc. It's used as a form of torture, so that says quite a lot about the effect it has on our senses, cognitive functions, decision-making, perspectives, memory, how we handle input, whether we can adequately process what's happened during the day and our overall health, mental and physical.

Not only is our sleep a boundary that we can assert and protect, being rested will help us to have the energy to assert boundaries in other areas of our lives. We can create bedtime routines, take breaks throughout our days, limit caffeine, remove as many electrical appliances from our rooms as possible, refrain from scrolling before bed or at the very least, pop on a blue-light filter.

Do Away with People-pleasing

Consistently trying to keep others happy is one of those areas where crossed wires can be rife. People-pleasers across the world will understand the conflict between the urge to be helpful, kind and generous and the resulting feelings of being taken for granted.

Being agreeable all of the time, over-accommodating, being over-apologetic, taking responsibility for how other people feel, chameleon behaviour, not speaking up when you feel sad, hurt or disappointed, avoiding arguments, basking in praise and not feeling able to say 'no', can create a horrible rod for our own backs — one that makes us feel overwhelmed, unseen, unheard and resentful.

The trouble with people-pleasing is that it places an onus on external validation and approval. It's those things that people-pleasers seek, and it's a hotbed for insecurity and low self-esteem because no matter which hoops we jump through, we can never keep everyone happy all of the time. Nor is it our place to try, or to take responsibility for the happiness of others. Becoming hyper-tuned-in to the needs of others typically means we grow out of tune with ourselves; we ignore the signs, the cues, the feelings and the instincts we have. It's unsustainable.

When this pattern of behaviour persists, we feel obliged and unduly influenced by the expectations and assumptions of others and our lives can feel out of control. Essentially, our lives *are* out of control because

'The trouble with people-pleasing is that it places an onus on external validation and approval.'

we're placing the reins in the hands of other people; we're allowing the way we spend our time and our behaviour to be heavily influenced by those we're seeking approval from.

Saying 'yes' to everyone else often means we're saying 'no' to ourselves. And there's nothing commendable in that, for we're their daughters, sons, mothers, fathers, sisters, brothers, friends and lovers too. We're liked, cared for, important and valued. We don't have to extinguish our flames to keep others shining brightly. When saying 'no' feels too icky, awkward or alien, try buying some time: 'Can I get back to you?' Practise speaking aloud your preferences when asked what you'd like to drink, watch, listen to, do, rather than the knee-jerk: 'I don't mind, what do you want to do?' Try not to answer a question asked of you with a question. Try to think of the 'no' to someone else as a glittering 'yes' to you; what can you do with that freer time, energy or headspace? What are the things on your Pinterest boards and webpage bookmarks that you've meant to do and haven't yet done? Which films, books and albums have you felt drawn to? What did you love to do as a child that got cast aside as adult life became fuller? What fills you up?

And remember: it's okay to set boundaries, to prioritise our safety and our mental health, to be a disappointment to others as long as we're not disappointed with ourselves, to be firm with our 'no's, to not know everything, to make mistakes, to disagree with the opinions, thoughts and ideas of other people.

'Saying "yes" to everyone else often means we're saying "no" to ourselves.'

Get Back in Touch with Yourself

When we become lax with our boundaries, our identity can merge with the identities of others, and we feel a bit lost, untethered and all at sea. We're not sure where our choices begin or end, who we are or what we genuinely like, love or dislike. We're not sure what lifts us or deflates us. It's that stuck feeling which can have us acting like a rabbit caught in the headlights; stunned, disorientated and confused.

If we've always relied on others to help us to understand who we are, then we can feel dependent and unable to stand alone. Healthy personal boundaries are when there's an expanse between who we are and who other people are. Our identity is something we hold steadfast to and dictates what our decisions might be. When we don't have that, we typically borrow or blend in with the identity of others.

It might be that we worry that if we start being who we are, we'll be rejected, so we layer the white lies on top of one another until even we become unsure of where we start and finish. Our sense of self can get worn down by life's challenges too; with grief, depression, violence and trauma, we can find ourselves longing for the pre-horrible-thing version of ourselves, grieving for who we once were.

It can feel as though we have got a blank canvas and no tools nor colour to fill it. The tools and colours are to hand. They just need dusting off and a little self-discovery.

Who Are You?

Building a sense of identity is like a jigsaw puzzle. Our identity is made up of so many different pieces: our personality traits, our beliefs, our qualities, what we look like, what we sound like, how we express ourselves, the things we feel drawn to or are interested in, the drinks we like to drink and the foods we want to eat, our culture and our biographies. We get to change the pieces as we change and evolve. We might find that we're passionate about a social cause and that forms part of our identity. We might try a new hobby and unearth something we thoroughly enjoy, or a hidden talent, and that shapes who we are. We might look through travel magazines and yearn for adventures or prefer our own space and sticking with what we know. We can meditate on the question 'Who am I?' and if that feels difficult, we can flip it on its head and start with 'Who am I not?' If you're not an unkind person, then you're probably kind. If you're not someone who loves networking or people in busy places, perhaps you're a nature-lover who prefers chilling at home with those closest to you, or alone.

Listen to the Warning Signs

Emotions, feelings, aches and pains, they're all the processing of data that tell us a story based on the way our brain assimilates our experiences (subconscious and conscious memories) and makes a prediction about what the outcome might be. That information then serves as a call to action to the rest of the body and provides us with physical, emotional, behavioural and cognitive cues: butterflies in our stomach, nausea, feeling edgy, hunger pangs, a shiver, headaches, flight or fight, shallow breathing, stomach and muscle aches and tightness, tension in our neck and shoulders, to name a few.

Our body tells us to pay attention and primes us to react in lots of different ways, but we typically quieten them or ignore them and plough on. When we feel uneasy and tense, that's a way that our body is communicating to us that we might be angry, stressed and/or be unwell. When we heed the signs, we can redress them throughout the day. Perhaps when our breathing becomes shallow, we might pause and take some long deep breaths. When we feel thirsty, we can have a drink.

What is your name?

_____

Who chose your name and why did they choose it?

_____

_____

Do you like your name? Why?

_____

_____

_____

My
superpower : _____ .

My Achilles
heel : _____ .

My hopes/fears

My favourite
lyric

63

Create a self-soothing toolkit to
help you through the tricky times.

4. Teaching our children (and our inner child) how to make space

When we reflect on our lives to date, it's the glorious and the grotty that spring to mind. The times that brought us great joy and the times which brought us pain. In truth, there's a myriad of 'grey'; the stuff that happened that didn't evoke such depths of emotion, the things we have to dig a bit deeper to uncover. It all plays a part in who we are now, the turning points in our lives and how we parent. And golly, this boundary work gets super-complicated when we are still learning about ourselves and are tasked with the role of teaching our dependants.

How we parent will be influenced by how we were parented, what we loved, what we hated, what we've witnessed from the behaviours and interactions of those around us, our life experiences since then, and a massive heap of outside unsolicited advice and judgement. It seems there's nothing more likely to stir up a hornet's nest than the sheer ferocity of some of these somewhat inflexible opinions as to what, as a parent, you should and shouldn't do. Aspersions are cast without rhyme or reason (which, in itself, is a lack of respect of boundaries) and it can be hard to trust our judgements and instincts.

When we were younger, we had caregivers who created boundaries for us. These boundaries were designed to keep us safe and to keep us well. They'd dish up meals they deemed to be suitable, create curfews and bedtime routines, and we followed their lead because that's what we're urged to do. At school, there was a framework to adhere to, too. We're taught classes for a curriculum designed by someone we'll never meet; there are rules we must follow, uniforms we must wear and a code of conduct that has us walking on the right-hand side of a corridor, holding doors open for adults and being kind, even to those who may not be kind to us. We weren't given a great deal of choice: told to share our toys, wear the clothes laid out for us, eat what's dished up and spend our weekends doing what's been decided by our parents.

All that is well and good until we get to the stage where we get to decide all of that. It can be quite scary to suddenly find ourselves without those boundaries and standing on our own two feet. On top of that, we might delve into the deep work of boundaries, only to find ourselves reverting to those old (sometimes not-so-healthy) family dynamics of yesteryear when we spend time with those we grew up with.

Parenting is always going to be a challenge, as we're trusted to teach things we mightn't yet have fully figured out. It's those judgement calls which are based on layers and layers of our own nurturing and experiences and boundary blocks. It's weighing up the things our parents taught us, with compassion because they too were teaching things they mightn't yet have fully figured out. It's adopting what worked 'well' and adapting the things that didn't. And even then, it's a matter of perspective. And oh boy, is it all emotive! A quick scroll on Mumsnet will show you just how emotive and heated conversations about our parenting choices can get. From the moment we tell people we're expecting, there's the unsought-after advice, the sharing of birth stories and the touching of our pregnant tums. Even writing a chapter on boundaries and parenting came with hesitation because it's bound to stir up mixed emotions – for all of us, whatever our experiences. But we start learning about boundaries when we're knee-high, so a book about boundaries without this chapter wouldn't make any sense. So much of boundary work is having uneasy conversations, with ourselves, and with others.

Added to that whirlpool of emotion is the contradiction of how we comfort, reassure and be fair in a world that can feel so cruel, scary and unfair. How do we instil a sense of safety and a sense of self alongside resilience and bounceback-ability? We mightn't have had the best of starts ourselves. If our childhood included trauma, neglect and pain, then boundaries have been obliterated from the off. Having to teach what we've not been taught can feel like walking on sand; unsure of our footing, scared of making mistakes and reopening wounds.

How then, do we navigate parenting in a way that keeps our children safe and also empowers them to have firm, healthy personal boundaries of their own? How do we create respect and understanding of boundaries and not resentment? How do we honour and work on our boundaries at the same time as we guide our children to acknowledge and work on theirs?

Empower Their No

Everything we teach our children has legs. How we respond to them as children sets the tone for how confident and empowered they feel in the future. Which, if we think about it too much, will send us in a tailspin. It's being mindful of the messages we're sending out and how they might translate in five, ten or twenty years' time. For example, if we constantly proclaim, 'Do as you're told', that becomes problematic when our children grow up to be adults and continue to 'do as they're told' when they're told – doing so could bring some pretty disastrous repercussions to the door. The same can be said when we ignore the awkwardness of a child when it comes to hugging or kissing a relative goodbye. If we urge them, despite their verbal and non-verbal protests to 'Go on, give Aunt Edna a kiss goodbye', it tells them that even if they don't want to let someone into their personal space, that they perhaps ought to do so if the other person wants them to and is relentless in their pursuit of it. That's downright dangerous.

'Intimacy should not be forced, nor should anyone be made to feel guilty for not wanting to let someone into their personal space.'

We can respect, honour and empower their 'no' by letting them know it's okay not to hug or kiss anyone they don't want to – it's an act of affection that absolutely should be given freely, as they see fit. Intimacy should not be forced, nor should anyone be made to feel guilty for not wanting to let someone into their personal space. As parents we can help enforce the 'no's in these situations, we can check our

'If we've been moulded to be obedient and compliant, then that's the behaviour that we continue with or take decades to unpick.'

responses and make sure that we don't emotionally manipulate the situation or let anyone else emotionally manipulate the situation.

We can check in too on our knee-jerk reactions when it comes to our children responding in the way we want them to – they're allowed to have boundaries with their parents, it's healthy. Breeding a generation of obedient and compliant children wipes out their natural appetite for learning. It's healthy to question, to challenge the status quo, to want to understand why. There's a slight pause between 'Right, it's time for bed' and 'Because I said so'. Offer explanations, reasonings and dialogues, rather than a 'my word is final' approach. Encourage the questioning in life of all things that feel unjust, unfair and wrong. Even if, to our perspective, they don't seem unjust, unfair or wrong. It's not about disempowering our 'no', either, it's about freeing up communication, so everyone gets clear on the 'why', explaining that there are limits and why these limits exist. Otherwise, there's no real opportunity to explore the reasoning behind boundaries. By the time we're older, and those opportunities present themselves, if we've been moulded to be obedient and compliant, then that's the behaviour that we continue with or take decades to unpick.

'Consistency
is key.'

There will be times when your 'no' is a 'no' even with all of the explanations, reasonings and dialogues: 'No, you can't bite your sibling', 'No, you can't hit the dog over the head with that', 'No, you can't see Mummy, she's having a rest'.

Empowering the 'no' of our children goes hand in hand with teaching them to respect the 'no' of others. It takes *cojones* sometimes, as parents, to keep a 'no' a 'no'. Children have tenacity in spades, and it can be wearing. They also, from a very early age, learn how to use emotion to sway things their way. Keeping the reasoned, calm and steadfast 'no' as it is after you've had every textbook 'Oooooh' and 'I hate you' and been through the crocodile tears helps teach our children to respect the boundaries of others. And consistency is key here, too.

Encourage Decision-making from an Early Age

So much of a child's life is made up of a routine they've had no say in. School uniforms, the school day, what they eat or drink, where they sit to eat it, what they learn, what they do at weekends, who they spend time with out of school, the time they go to bed and so on.

There's little opportunity for them to hone their decision-making and problem-solving skills – vital attributes for this adulting lark. There's not much room for them to have a say, to explore and express and make decisions beyond who they're friends with, what toys they want to play with and what they want to watch on TV. Without being allowed to make decisions wider than that, they lose the lessons that come with deliberating, weighing up options, dealing with consequences and those not-so-nice 'learning from your mistakes' situations. And then comes that time at secondary school where you're expected to make massive decisions about what you'd like to do for the rest of your life. Those decisions are 100 per cent on you, and it can feel like you've been handed a tremendous weight of responsibility that you feel ill-equipped for. You might look to your friends, your parents and your teachers for advice, but ultimately, only you can decide what's next.

So how can we bridge that gap? How can we scatter choices throughout their lives so that the arrival of adulthood isn't such a rude awakening?

We can honour their self-expression by providing freedom of choice. Let them choose what they wear outside of school. We can involve them in the consultation as to what weekend plans, or holiday plans, might be. We can allow them to change their minds and make room for them to evolve, even if it's in an unexpected way that screws with our identity-related boundary clocks. We can be mindful of the rhetoric surrounding people who seem different to us in the way they look or sound and make sure that our children's questions aren't shut down. We can listen and not assume that just because we're older, that we're smarter than they are – we can learn a great deal from their insights. We can stop speaking over them and make space at the table for their input and perceptions and opinions and insights. We can apologise to them when we've made a mistake and openly admit that we were wrong. When they come to us with problems, we can stop with the 'fixing' and inspire them to start thinking of solutions.

Respect Their Privacy

When we pick our children up from school or childcare, they're not always tripping over themselves to chat about their day. They're exhausted and what feels like need-to-know information for us is part of their day-to-day. We can lay the foundations for the boundaries surrounding their personal space, including headspace, and their privacy by not firing a million questions at them. The details tend to filter out at mealtimes, or when getting ready for bed, or during an unrelated conversation.

A gaggle of children can bring out revered diplomacy skills as we teach our own to be kind, to be respectful and to consider the feelings of others. Sharing toys is where things can get a bit fraught. It's an odd one this sharing toys thing because it can blur the lines of ownership; this is mine, and that's yours – that's the basis of excellent boundary work – and the ability to be able to distinguish between the two. It stands to reason that our belongings are ours to do with as we wish, right?! Yet we so often encourage our children to share their toys if they don't want to. Isn't it up to them what they do with their toys? Just as it's up to us what we do with our stuff? We sometimes tie the actions of our children in with who we are as parents. We're proud when they do the things we consider noble and cringe when the opposite is true. It sometimes blinkers us to the core message – what do we want to teach, or learn, here in this moment? Nobody has to share anything they don't want to share if it's theirs: toys, food, personal space, money, thoughts, time, clothes, etc. If we teach our children that, then they'll learn to share, or not, on their own merits and most importantly, to share because they want to and not because they feel they have to.

Speaking of sharing thoughts, this is another dilly-dally of boundary-testing and honouring trust. As our children grow older, the stakes of the 'need-to-know information' can feel higher. Our natural instincts to keep our loved ones safe can have us imagining a whole host of unsavoury scenarios – this is normal. It's also normal to have an urge to find out more, and this is where boundaries can get a bit squiffy again.

Rationally, and morally, we shouldn't ever read our child's diary or texts nor rummage through their bags. Their private thoughts are just that, private. The act of exploring those thoughts by writing them down and expressing them is powerful. To casually read anyone's diary is an infringement of privacy. Full stop. It just is. We all deserve personal private space that's respected. Those of us who had that privacy invaded will remember how it damaged the trust we had with our parents or friends. So if we do decide to break that trust, it can't be a decision we take lightly. It has to be backed up by real concern for their safety and wellbeing, and only then.

Don't Forget What it Was Like to Be a Child

There's a sense of wonder and curiosity that comes from being a child. Our imaginations conjure up all sorts of magical and mystical scenarios. There's a thirst for understanding the world around us, resulting in the endless 'But, why?' questions. We have a world inside of our heads that isn't yet filled with responsibility, one that's rich with unicorns, slaying dragons, monster Lego plans and fairy tales. Hours can be whiled away reading, listening to music, playing with slime, drawing, colouring and inventing games with friends.

The thirst for knowledge can be a trifle overwhelming for us parents: *Are we there yet? But, why? Why? Why?* We don't always have the answers, and in the constant life juggle where it feels as though everything is demanding our attention, the 'whys' can be tiresome. They're tiresome because they're flung at us so often, they're tiresome because we have to try and verbalise concepts in a way that a young person might comprehend and they're tiresome because they force a pause when we already feel overwhelmed and time-poor. We don't want to dampen their inquisitive nature, but equally, we have heads full of adulting thoughts which often take us away from the present moment.

But do you remember, when you were younger, that little lift that came with learning something new? That portal into a world that you'd not had access to, which feels so enchanting once you've got the key. The real need to get your bearings and to have an inkling into what's happening or what to expect.

Questioning the status quo is questioning boundaries in progress. It's a super-handy tool for us to have as adults as it's the only way systems, processes and laws are changed.

When we're in the car, and the questions are competing with tunes on the radio, and we can't think for the sound around us, we can offer an option – music or questions? Perhaps too, we can pre-empt their 'Are we there yet?' queries with regular updates as to where we are and how long is left of the journey – it's this kind of information we hold in our heads anyway. After all, we,

'Questioning the status quo is questioning boundaries in progress.'

as adults, like to know the answers to those questions ourselves.

When it comes to those more serious questions about death, sex, sexuality, race, homelessness, crime, the world around us, it does us well to remember that to a child, those questions come from the same place of curiosity as when they wanted to know what noise a cow made. The questions they ask about those topics feel to them no different from the questions they ask about anything else. It's how we react to the questions asked of us and how we craft the answers that matters. Age-appropriate knowledge sometimes comes into play here, and it's a fine art between that and remaining honest in what is an opportunity to broaden their awareness and acceptance on important topics.

Help Them to Dial into Their Needs

When babies are born, they have a really handy way of expressing that they need something – they cry. And they cry loudly. We become attuned to the different tones of crying, too; the cry of hunger might be ever so slightly of a different tone to the call for a hug, for example. They unashamedly ask for what they want.

Something strange happens to us between that phase – where we instinctually express our needs – and when we become adults. Taking what we need and communicating what we need becomes something we're not always confident in doing. We've unlearned how to do it along the way.

As parents, then, we can look back on our experiences and identify the times our needs went unheeded and when perhaps they were invalidated and silenced. We can reflect on the times we felt heard, seen and happy too. In doing so, we can use those experiences and calibrate how we might parent our children so that they grow to understand the importance of their needs, and at the same time respect the needs of others. We can embolden our children to continue to communicate how they are feeling, rather than putting words into their mouths. We can help them delve into why they might be angry, sad, worried, overwhelmed, tired or scared, and to hold space no matter how uncomfortable that may be at times. We can assist them in exploring what they need at that point, whether that be some comforting, cognitive tools, reassurance or action. The opposite is also true: what makes them happy, laugh, feel comforted, excited and supported? Encourage more of that too.

It's healthy to talk about this stuff, to open the door for the vulnerability that so often gets locked away and to do so by leading by example – sharing our experiences with them, talking about how we feel, and why, and making room for our needs. It's not building a 'snowflake generation' to enable dialogue about the power of our emotions, to hold space for people to explore their feelings, to advocate kindness, self-care, self-expression and parity of esteem. If we want to raise kids to be confident, mentally and physically healthy, resilient and kind, then we need to teach them how to vocalise so much that goes unsaid. To heed their needs in a world that wants to take so much more from them.

Widen Their Awareness

We only know what we know. And, as children, we only know what those around us have introduced us to: cultures, people from different walks of life, lifestyles, social causes, hobbies, food, music, adventure, etc. We can sometimes have a narrow viewpoint of the world because it's never been extended outwards and is made up of the people around us, what they're like, what they do, how they've treated us and how they treat other people.

We wouldn't have Serena Williams – top extraordinary tennis player – if she hadn't at some point picked up a tennis racquet and ball and then trained her socks off. The same can be said for humanitarians, actors, musicians, scientists, artists, plumbers, chefs, bakers, graphic designers, writers, all professions. Something, however minute it might have seemed, piqued their interests and they had the space to learn more about it.

The world is rich in differences, and it's crucial that we grow up understanding not only that those differences exist, but that it's okay for us to be different from what's and who's around us. Also that fundamentally, we're all similar in our inherent needs. Labels are for jars, not people. We're complex, we can be many things all at once, and if we're told something often enough, then we start to believe it. *You're not good at this, and you struggle with that, you're never going to be able to ... those things don't happen for people like us.* Let's not pigeonhole ourselves or our children. Let's not create mental boundaries and blocks needlessly. Let's not clip their wings, trample on their sense of adventure, suffocate their imagination or dampen their enthusiasm.

'Labels are for jars, not people.'

'Within all of us is   There are thousands of examples
untapped potential.'   of people smashing through glass
                                            ceilings, doing extraordinary
never-been-done-before things. Who are we to say what a child
can or can't become?

Within all of us is untapped potential, things we're drawn to,
opportunities we're not aware of yet and skills we've honed after
years and years of practice.

Remember that Our Actions Speak Loudly

Words are powerful when followed through with meaning and
intent. The power sits in the aftermath when our words are
followed by aligned action and consequences. We need to believe
what we're saying in order for others to believe us. That then
needs to be backed up with the action or consequences that
follow next.

The non-verbal way we communicate says so much more than
the words that fall out of our mouths about what we will and won't
tolerate. Our body language, facial expressions and the tone of
voice we use. How we react in certain situations and whether we
mean what we say and say what we mean. Our sincerity, surety
and confidence. Our uncertainty and inauthenticity.

When our words and actions don't match up, it's confusing
for everyone around us. We say one thing when we mean, or do,
another. For our children, this causes them to feel insecure and
sometimes, unsafe. As parents (and as people, in general), we
need to walk our walk and talk our talk because those around us

are watching and taking it all in. They're learning behaviour from the things they see us do.

If we stress the importance of heeding their needs but at the same time we run ourselves ragged – our actions are at odds with our words. If we encourage our children to say 'no' when we continually, to our own detriment, say 'yes' – then we're sending mixed messages. The same applies when we say 'no' to our children but it's not a good solid 'no' – if it's an unsure one, they can sense that. They'll naturally push back against the boundaries we set if we don't assert them surely, or if we're unsure as to why we're asserting something in the first place. Our actions speak loudly; they underline the messages and teachings we're hoping to pass on to those within our care. When we do so clearly and consistently and mindfully, we show our children how to do the same and how to confidently create healthy boundaries.

Retain, and Work On, Your Sense of Identity

Many parents feel as though they lose a sense of themselves when they become parents. Not helped at all by the constant references to them as 'Thingymebob's Mummy or Daddy'. Having a baby changes our focus; we've got to keep a little 'un safe, and the weight of that responsibility is one we feel palpably. Then when they're old enough to start school, we still need to be flexible and work around their school day and holidays and illnesses.

A study that was commissioned by the Association of Accounting Technicians found that the average adult deals with

'Your feelings matter, whatever they are.' 109 life admin tasks a year.[7] Life admin includes: applying for a job, writing a CV, completing tax returns, booking appointments, paying bills, buying gifts, buying a new home, dealing with insurance and so on. What that doesn't take into consideration is the sheer mental load of the day-to-day; the washing, the dishes, the food shop, the preparation and planning of meals and oh-so-much that seems to happen on autopilot or by the magic laundry bunny. When we have children, that's turbo-charged. Mixed with the sleep deprivation, it can feel nigh-on impossible to carve out time for anything other than all of the caring and preparing. We're sucked into all of the doing, and even though it comes from a place of love, it can still feel monotonous and all-encompassing.

It can feel nigh-on impossible to reclaim any chunk of time, it really can, and asking for help can feel dogged by those self-shaming thoughts of 'I should be able to cope'. Asking for help doesn't mean we're not coping; it means we can cope with more. The saying 'It takes a village to raise a child' is a true one. It's also true that not all of us have a village to hand. But we can build one, seek one out, join one and be open to having help and support. We lose our identity when our entire world and purpose merge into being parents. If we don't ever have the opportunity to be 'Thingymebob's Mummy or Daddy' plus something else, then we're naturally going to feel one-dimensional. There's room (albeit not so much room) for us to be as dimensional as we want

---

7 Source: https://www.aat.org.uk/news/article/aat-research-adults-carry-out-109-'life-admin'-tasks-every-year

to be. The backlash is that being a parent is the most special role in the world, and it *is* a privilege and a blessing. But we can also want to have other stuff going on besides, and that's okay, just as it's okay if we don't want to have other stuff going on. Your feelings matter, whatever they are – they're valid, even when you're a parent.

Your sense of identity isn't usually lost; it's buried beneath the demands on and of you. Whether you consciously make space for self-care; time with friends, old hobbies, new hobbies, time to get dressed, a non-interrupted shower or bath, a haircut, to sleep; or add the foods you love to the food shop even if nobody else likes them and upgrade your tatty slippers, don't forget to take care of yourself and to do the things (whatever they are) that comfort, reassure and nurture you, too.

Write a letter to your inner child.

What wonky messaging have you heard?

Have you constructed any barricades? What are they?

How I feel (a)	How I want to feel (b)	What action will take me from (a) to (b)?

5. Making space within relationships

Relationships are the coming together of people who have different habits, tendencies, personalities, emotional baggage, problems, beliefs, experiences and perspectives, but who are all trying to navigate life in the best way they can.

If we've never been taught this boundary malarkey, then we might infer that to create boundaries within a relationship when we're so used to hearing crappy hyperbole such as, 'What's theirs is mine and what's mine is theirs' or 'Best friends for ever', is selfish, heavy-handed, businesslike and cumbersome.

Quite the contrary is true. Boundaries harness trust, intimacy and honesty; they de-blur the lines that sometimes rob us of a sense of who we are on our own merits. When we build our identity around our relationship to someone else – somebody's partner, somebody's parent, somebody's friend – we diminish the vastness, the complexity, the nuances, the potential of who we are and who we might grow into.

Boundaries come into play from the get-go. From the very beginning of a relationship, we convey verbally and non-verbally our boundaries; what we're willing to tolerate, what's right and wrong for us, our likes and dislikes, how we communicate and how respectful we are, or aren't. There are endless opportunities to assert, flex and bin our limits and it doesn't matter whether those interactions stem from sitting together in class at school, finding ourselves at adjoined desks at work or from a dating app; we continuously have the chance to demonstrate, address and adjust our messaging.

The media we consume paints these compelling masterpieces of how a relationship should or could be: the intimate looks, the romantic gestures, the friends who drop everything to be by your side, the parents who have it all figured out and give such sage spot-on advice. That's without the social comparison we painfully put ourselves through; the 'life benchmarks' we might not be anywhere near but everyone else seems to be cruising through like some box-ticking exercise. The dreamy marriage proposals, the vomit-less pregnancy, the beaming and bouncing babies, the friendships which have traversed adolescence, long distances, holidays and other people coming into their lives. We forget that what we see in the media isn't necessarily true or real or particularly representative. We forget that social media, and social interactions in real life, are edited and curated; we all paint a picture we want people to see and it's not often the full picture of what's going on for us.

When we compare the highlights reel of the people in our feeds (because that's pretty much what social media is) to our reality, it's skewed well out of our favour. The comparison between carefully edited, really well-considered photos and captions, and our own reality can make our relationships seem lacking, dull and ungratifying, creating unrealistic expectations which damage our 'real-life' relationships – not ever really giving them a fair chance.

'Boundaries are the underbelly of what nourishes a relationship.'

What all of our meaningful relationships have in common is that they require maintenance to keep them meaningful: time, commitment, ongoing support, attention, effort, mutual trust, affection and respect, the willingness to work together and write a new page when it's become problematic to reside where you are. None of that sounds particularly compelling, dazzling or adventurous but boundaries are the underbelly of what nourishes a relationship way past the exciting and magnetic sunshine-rainbows-butterflies-in-your-belly-knees-a'-wobbling stages. Healthy long-lasting relationships are fed, watered and cultivated, continually and consciously.

These relationships of ours can be long-lasting like those we have with our siblings, our parents, our children, friendships or of the romantic kind. They can also be shorter term such as those we have with teachers, employers, employees or professional partnerships. They can be fleeting too: the there's-not-going-to-be-a-second-first-date, the conversations we might have as we're served in a bakery or waiting for a bus, that knowing nod in a packed university lecture or the unity we experience at a concert, play or sporting event.

It doesn't matter how long term or fleeting, these varying interactions leave their mark on us – even the 'blink and it's over' ones. Consider being the recipient of a random act of kindness and the emotion that would evoke. Then consider being the victim of a crime and how terrifying and invasive that would feel. The actual interaction itself mightn't have lasted long but the effects of it could last a lifetime. The things we do or say will be remembered long after we've moved on.

It's complicated to know when to give space, when to make space and when to lean. Holding on to our sense of individual identity whilst fostering a relationship identity is one of the hardest things to do. And whilst there's typically a merging of physical assets after a while, holding on to our sense of self can feel like holding back or as though we're not open to intimacy.

Communicate, Communicate, Communicate

Communication is something we underestimate. After all, going over scenarios in our heads means we often put a lot of thought and mental effort into understanding, predicting and planning. We forget that other people can't read our minds in the same way that we can't read theirs. When we communicate clearly, consistently and honestly, we find that boundaries de-fuzz. After all, we've all experienced a time when we've said 'yes' to a request of our time, energy, money when really we've meant to say 'no'.

'When we communicate clearly, consistently and honestly, we find that boundaries de-fuzz.'

That comes at a cost, not just to our resources but it dents our relationships ever so slightly. Unintentionally, we've missed out on the chance to be honest, to speak our mind. Unless we're willing to verbalise our needs and wants, nobody will ever know what they are. If we're begrudgingly doing something for someone else, we're not giving our resources freely. That tips the scales and leads to resentment the other person isn't even aware of.

Communication isn't just in the words we say; so much of it is also non-verbal. The non-verbal tends to reinforce the words we're uttering: our facial expressions, hand gestures and body language are typically congruent with what we're verbalising, and this really helps when we're explaining and asserting our boundaries.

Communicating and enforcing our boundaries are where the difficulty lies for many of us; we fear confrontation, we don't want to appear awkward or put people out, nor are we always well-versed in voicing our thoughts, wants and needs or in making ourselves heard and understood.

Being clear on our boundaries isn't just healthy for us, it's healthy for those around us too because our levels of tolerance and ability to determine what's acceptable and not acceptable vary – to know this, we need to be told this. It clears up misunderstanding, confusion and conflict and manages expectations about our limits and values. It fosters integrity and trust and words can be taken at face value rather than having underlying unclear and unfair context.

When we're in the middle of a disagreement, or indeed when we sense one coming, we might pull up the drawbridge. There's a difference between wanting to make space to reflect, perhaps to calm down and to gather our thoughts, and doing it to evade and block communication, effectively putting up a wall to block out other perspectives, grievances and thoughts – not conducive to a healthy, well-balanced relationship. In disallowing the opportunity to listen and properly hear each other, we open the door to passive aggression, resentment, mental exhaustion and issues being swept under the carpet or becoming the elephant in the room, all of which can put a colossal dent in the longevity of the relationship. Dealing with disagreements as and when they arise provides everyone with the opportunity to convey their needs, and for expectations to be renegotiated with clarity and compassion and a shared willingness to listen, to hear and not just awaiting a turn to speak.

Take Responsibility, but Not for Everything

When we point the finger elsewhere and lay blame at someone else's door, then we're disempowering ourselves; we're handing over our self-control, our autonomy, our choices and our decisions. It's how we get stuck in a rut – by dancing to the tune of another and growing bored by it. We're not puppets on a string, here to live a life that someone else has visualised and created; we totally get a say in what we do, how we do it, why we do it and when we do it. Bending and swaying to the demands and expectations of other people is a sure-fire way to *lose our way*. Important cognitive skills like logic and reasoning atrophy from lack of use.

The reverse is also true; when someone repeatedly points the finger of blame in our direction, they're not taking responsibility for their behaviour, choices and thoughts. We don't have control, or shouldn't have any control, over their behaviour because healthy boundaries create a space between their identity and ours; where we begin and end, and where they begin and end.

Taking responsibility for our actions and our choices and the subsequent consequences means that we don't lay any of that at someone else's door. The same can be said for taking on other people's responsibilities: in doing so, we're infringing on their boundaries – even if it totally seems to serve them that way, it won't in the long term. Boundaries help us to take care of ourselves, but they also encourage and enable other people to learn to take care of themselves. Cohabiting doesn't have to equal co-dependence.

We Can't Fix Everything and Everyone

The solutions to other people's problems always seem so clear, so darned obvious and that's because we can look at them with less emotion – you see, emotional reactions aren't always rational ones. When we derive our happiness from how happy or unhappy the people around us are, we're naturally going to switch to fixing mode so that we can feel happy again and boy, do we like to feel helpful. The trouble with that is that we're taking on stuff when it's not our place to do so. It's an almighty infringement of boundaries – we might have the best of intentions but unless we've been asked for help, helping isn't always helpful or kind, even when it *feels* helpful and kind. Whether it's unsolicited advice, lending money that we'll never ask for back or taking ownership of all the solution-based thinking, that's doing ourselves and the other person such a disservice – even though it doesn't feel that way. We're forgetting that space between us and other people. We're ignoring the self-work that needs to be done – by them and by us. Our happiness is our responsibility, and only ours. In tying our reactions and attitude and happiness to that of another, we're doing away with boundaries.

It does feel great to be of help, to be able to assist, to iron out wrinkles and crinkles for another. However, what has worked for us may not work for someone else; our answer might not be their answer. Life is full of twists and turns and hurdles and obstacles, and that will never change, it's the nature of the beast. When we do our best to pave the way and lay out a metaphorical plush red carpet for someone, we're doing the donkey work, we're drawing on our experiences and we're carving a path we've deemed to be the right one. All of this denies them the opportunity to experience the change-prompting pain that comes from getting so fed up with the chaos, the drama and the discomfort, to reach the pain point where the only conceivable action is to alter something, to find solutions and then to be victorious in their own right, to try on a solution for size and accept or deny it and repeat over and over, and to bear the consequences of their own thoughts, attitudes and actions – all stuff that's confidence-building, resilience-building and transferable to every area of our lives.

Being the white knight over and over and over again breeds a sense of helplessness in others and a dependency that can later on, down the line, cause disdain and resentment. Let people grow at the rate, and in the ways, that are right for them.

And of course, this also means that we need to recognise when we defer to the 'fixers' in our lives instead of looking to ourselves to discover a resolution in the first instance. The times we hope people will fight our battles for us, or perhaps on social media when we bolster a pack mentality against someone who has caused us upset. Relying on others to meet our emotional needs or to fix us is a violation of their boundaries and ours, and any third party who might get swept up in the middle of it all.

Get Used to Resistance

When we experience change, we can feel the internal resistance to it. Even if the change is fresh and exciting, we tend to return to baseline behaviours when we're up against it; busy, fatigued, stressed. Our brain operates happily at our baseline, it prefers things to stay easy and the same, it likes patterns – including those of behaviour. Change then, is always a challenge. For many of us, too, it can evoke a fear of the unknown and also draws on additional cognitive function: it feels as though we're going against the grain and to some intents and purposes, we are. We're going against internal and external conditioning which will naturally take some time and patience to undo and redo.

Once we set down this path of boundary work, the inner resistance can present itself in these multiple persuasive and self-doubting thoughts: 'Am I being selfish?', 'But I really like helping other people', 'Maybe I should just …', 'I'm making this all about me, me, me', 'This is going to go down like a lead balloon'. And so on, and so on and on it goes like a broken internal record. These thoughts don't half put into question why we're bothering to change but undermine our confidence and self-worth at the same time.

The important factor behind any change, big or small, is the 'why' – understanding the need for the change. Once we've clarity here, we have a rational answer to those somewhat irrational thoughts which are bred from caring what other people think about us, from fear of their reactions and uneasiness in trying on this boundary stuff for size. Boundary work is built upon the repeated rehearsing and practising and asserting and following through on the consequences. What other people think of us isn't really any of our business; we're judged whether we do or whether we don't. The only approval that matters is that of our own. We have to be able to look in the mirror and know that we're doing ourselves justice.

The resistance doesn't just come from within, either. This finding-change-uncomfortable thing is universal, in that we like to know what to expect as much as is possible, and some people have a low tolerance to change. Rejigging our boundaries can be met with some external resistance because they, more frequently than not, change the dynamics of our relationships. And that's completely understandable, and often navigable with clear communication and explanation. We might experience resistance to the change in other people too, as they seek to understand and solidify their boundaries.

There are times that our boundaries are met with an emotional response and whilst that can be extremely distressing and icky, we have zilch control over how people will react. Unacceptance of our boundaries from others does not mean that we're

'Boundary work is built upon the repeated rehearsing and practising and asserting.'

being unacceptable, that we have to change our minds. You can be the most generous, kind-spirited, warm-hearted, loveliest of people and still say no. Upholding a no when needed stops our yeses being taken advantage of. Newly found boundaries often highlight the people in our lives who prospered from our having none. The resistance can be symptomatic of their self-interest. Their reaction says so little about our boundaries but quite a lot about their character, their lofty expectations of us and what they stand to lose when we get our boundaries into shape. It's a lose-lose game when we have no boundaries, remember that. We all deserve to be happy but not at the expense of another person's happiness. The adverse reaction often expresses that, for that particular person, they would be quite content to be happy at our expense. Well, no more.

'Upholding a no when needed stops our yeses being taken advantage of.'

Do Take No for an Answer

No means no and that's the beginning, middle and end of it. To encourage people not to take no for an answer, which is so often the rhetoric linked with tenacity, striving and achieving, is downright dangerous. No is a complete sentence which requires no explanation and should absolutely be taken at face value. So many of us feel uneasy saying no in the first place; conditioning means that we feel a nuisance, rude, disempowered and that's the easy bit, really. Keeping our intended 'no' a no, when we're on the receiving end of a relentless inability to accept it as such, can wear us down, undermine our confidence and put our safety into question – that's the really tough part. It's two sides of the same coin; growing in confidence to assert our 'no' no matter the consequence is important – but as a society, too, we need to learn to teach our children from a very young age that no quite simply, but powerfully, means no in all interactions with other people.

Accepting a 'no' is absolutely not the same as bounce-back-ability, overcoming obstacles or finding an alternative path when it comes to our careers or activism or seeking changes in our society; but when it comes to interpersonal relationships, no is a no is a no is a no is a no.

Don't Scatter Your Yeses Around Like Confetti

A yes is often anything but. It can be a 'maybe later' or it can be an 'I'd really rather not' or it can be a resounding 'no'. Yet what squeaks out of our mouths is a 'yes' that's laden with everything it isn't. Imagine how much more straightforward our lives would be if our yeses were well-considered and certain. Imagine how much healthier our relationships might be if we really could take people at their word. Imagine too, how much stress, awkwardness and backtracking we'd be free from.

For as useful and indispensable as we might want to feel or believe we are, what's really, truly valued and integral to healthy, balanced relationships is honesty. People who really care about us would rather we were upfront, honest and not tying ourselves up in knots. And that's the cinch, isn't it?! That's the painful part that we'll all have experienced or will experience – people come into our lives and the relationship is wonky-tonk. Those feelings, the ones we feel of love, respect, care and compassion, aren't always reciprocated. It begs the question: why are we giving away our yeses to those people? The ones we know, deep down, wouldn't help us, who would rather we were burnt out keeping their needs met than contemplate our own. Strong, thriving relationships include give and take. If one person is always giving and another always taking, then we're going to end up with one person on their knees with nothing left to give and another hopping and skipping and jumping with vitality for life.

Those yeses of ours are valuable because they're a gift of our resources to another. Don't scatter them around like confetti, take time to appreciate the emotional, mental, physical, spiritual, financial and time cost of that ever-so-precious yes, and make sure that a) we're topped up enough to be able to afford dipping into that resource, and that b) our 'yes' is an unequivocal 'yes' without strings attached.

What About Compromise, Though?

All relationships require us to compromise. The tricky bit? Being compromising without compromising ourselves. Without giving up the things which are most important to us. Not shelving our needs, wants and dreams to ease the tension created in having a conversation where compromise is the goal – that's just delaying the friction and resentment which is bound to pop its head up again at a later date. Putting our needs, wants and dreams to one side isn't compromise unless there is mutuality and reciprocity at

'The best relationships are supportive, value equity and fairness, and make space for all that's important to one another.'

play. The best relationships are supportive, value equity and fairness, and make space for all that's important to one another.

Compromise can be reached by both parties listening and discussing within the realms of their boundaries, those limits of which we've identified and aligned, to preserve and support our whole selves. If the trade-off is one that calls into question our integrity and self-identity, then it's conceding and not compromising. If a relationship constantly fails you, it's got boundary issues.

What a well-rounded discussion does is cut out the crap: the guilt-tripping, the coercion, blackmail, belittling, gaslighting, bringing up the past, pulling other people in to side with us; not place a greater emphasis on one person's needs over another. Compromise stems from a willingness to find a solution that's of mutual benefit, one that considers the health of the relationship as a sum of two individual parts coming together, and navigating boundaries for the strength of a relationship.

Walking Away is an Option, Sometimes the Only One

We invest a great deal of ourselves into a valued relationship and when we deliberately turn our back on it, it's often not just the person we're taking into consideration, it's the cost of the relationship to us – the weight of what we've invested into it and the bits of ourselves we may have lost or will lose. Walking away sounds so easy but it's anything but. Especially when we're experiencing shame, guilt, a myriad of emotions and feelings. We might have assets, sometimes dependants to consider. It's the giving up of a vision we once held for ourselves, something we wholeheartedly bought into with everything we had, and everything we were, and stepping into the unknown. But we can re-frame walking away and consider what might we be walking towards, instead. Perhaps freedom, peace, a future that lights us up instead of a life that tears us down.

Relationships are changeable in the same way we evolve as individuals and sometimes, we might grow apart rather than together. There are times when our values and perspectives and who we are and where we see ourselves heading become so misaligned that a relationship becomes a detrimental one. Some relationships are doomed from the outset but not all toxic relationships start out that way – some relationships morph into being unhealthy, unsupportive and unkind.

What does a toxic relationship feel like? It feels imbalanced, uncomfortable, unsteady and unstable, as though we're walking on eggshells and all of the compromises that entails. Toxicity can be subtle; it can creep in slowly and quietly, it can be laced with smiles, apologies and remorse, and it can also have bells and whistles and be downright dangerous. Some hallmarks include: a lack of trust, nonstop criticism and judgement, guilt-tripping, never-ending disagreement and failure of the ability to see eye to eye, withdrawal of affection, senseless jealousy, perpetual lying, gaslighting, constant belittling and name-calling, abusive behaviour, the threat of violence, love feeling as though it's conditional and comes with caveats, a lack of balance with one person's needs prioritised above another's, disrespect, constant drama, a tug-of-war for control, a feeling of negativity, isolating you from friends and family, damaging your self-worth and confidence, pretence and then some.

A toxic, unhealthy and unkind relationship is one which stunts our personal growth, one within which it feels difficult to thrive and bloom. Quite often, it's one where someone is putting up and shutting up about big or small stuff that's compromising and oppressing their safety and self-identity; emotionally, mentally, physically and spiritually.

When we get to a point where no amount of communicating nor boundary-setting and asserting seems to address those gaping cracks, something has to change. Other people's behaviour is outside our control, it's not in our remit or power to change other people. What is in our control is our reactions and subsequent courses of action.

It's the ultimate creation of a boundary: to acknowledge that a relationship is troubled beyond repair and to construct space and distance there.

What aren't you communicating, and to whom?

_____ .

_____ .

_____ .

_____ .

_____ .

_____ .

_____ .

_____ .

What do you need to start taking responsibility for?

Times I've said 'yes' but it was really a 'no'	Next time I'll say ...

6. Making space in a digital age

If life feels rambunctious, fast and furious, then we can look to the technology at our fingertips for some of the answers to the increasing pace of our days and ways. Specifically, our smartphones and any device which allows us to access information and communicate electronically and digitally.

A telephone is no longer a telephone. In fact, in a day where there seems to be a leaning towards texting and not talking, it's a fair assessment to say that a mobile telephone isn't used as initially designed any more. Long gone are the days we'd hold on until 6 p.m., when the cheaper calls kicked in on our landlines, and spend the following hours chatting frenetically to the people we'd spent all day with at school. Plans would be set in stone as there was no way to contact someone if they weren't at home or near a payphone. We'd have to either memorise our friend's telephone numbers (which might've been as short as four digits if they lived in the same town as you) or look for their telephone number in the phone book – as long as they weren't ex-directory. Dial-up internet dialled up the phone bills and came with a particular static and interference sound that we early MSN adopters will remember with fondness, recalling all too well how we'd sit with our fingers crossed that a connection would indeed be made. Download speeds were at a snail's pace compared to today's standards but the excitement was unrivalled that we could download anything at all. Even then, we didn't know how good we'd got it.

Our Human Need to Share

In both Indonesia and in southern Europe cave paintings have been discovered that have been dated to around 40,000 years old. These paintings are thought to illustrate some of the oldest types of written communication, as symbols and pictographs.

From pictographs to carvings on rock or bone, marking rockfaces by whatever means, including scratching, carving, chiselling, drilling and engraving, dating back to approximately 12,000 years ago or older, these petroglyphs seem to communicate territories, depict terrain and have a spiritual or religious significance.

When it comes to the oldest of old-school ways of communicating long distance, then we can look to smoke signals for that. These signals were used to broadcast information to other people, and the number of puffs of smoke meant different things. Eventually, a system was devised which represented the alphabet. It wasn't just used by the Native Americans or the soldiers positioned at the Great Wall of China, either. Smoke is still used today to signal the selection of a new Pope by the Vatican, and the military use smoke grenades to indicate positions and to signal for help.

For even longer distances, messenger pigeons, which later became known as pigeon post, have been used for well over 2000 years. The Romans used them and before that the Greeks used them to carry news of the winners of the ancient Olympics. In the nineteenth century Paul Julius Reuter, the founder of Reuters news agency, used pigeons to carry information about stock market prices. Pigeons were used in both world wars and three individual messenger birds were awarded the Dickin Medal, given to animals which displayed particular courage in wartime.

Known for their fantastic sense of direction and 'homing' instincts, pigeons were trained to deliver messages, reliably and over a considerable distance. It wasn't until 2002 that the police pigeon service in Orissa, northeast India, was finally disbanded.

The earliest known written text artefact, signalling the invention of a formal writing system, dates back to around 5000 years ago. Writing brought with it the first means by which couriers would transport letters from one place to another by horse and carriage. Different countries had differing systems which evolved into what we know it as today: snail mail. The method by which we can send letters, parcels and packages to anywhere in the world. So called owing to its relative speed when compared to the speed of sending an email.

Where prior forms of communication might take weeks or even months to reach the intended recipient, the invention of the telegraph in the early 1800s – the transmission of electrical signals, using Morse code, over telegraph lines – meant that not only could communication happen over long distances, it could do so much more easily and quickly.

Alexander Graham Bell made the first-ever telephone call in

1876 and in the same way that we're now trying to get to grips with the internet and all that entails, the telephone was met with tremendous excitement but also fears that it would threaten privacy, lead to more sophisticated crime and destroy jobs. Landlines become mainstream in the early 1900s. In 1973 Dr Martin Cooper, who worked at Motorola, made the first public phone call from a mobile device.

The internet as we know it today, the World Wide Web, was born in 1989 and since then it's as if we've pressed 'fast forward' in how quickly the landscape has changed. It's been one hell of a rollercoaster ride from then to now. Communication has become as instantaneous as the internet connection is strong, largely due to the Simon Personal Communicator, invented by IBM in 1992 – what you and I would now call a 'smartphone'. Add social networking to the mix, and we end up where we are now; with communication turbo-charged and us in desperate need of a re-charge.

You see, all of this opportunity and widening of our horizons comes at a cost. Social media is designed to be addictive; it's in the interest of the companies who develop and create these platforms that we spend a lot of time on them. There's a dopamine hit we receive when our posts are liked, shared and applauded.[8] We have access to the edited and intimate details of people's lives like never before which can cause a sense of not being enough nor doing enough, particularly on our very worst days.

Movements can reach many more people, leading to substantial

---

8 Source: http://sitn.hms.harvard.edu/flash/2018/dopamine-smartphones-battle-time/

shifts in social change – for the better, and the worse. Trolling and cyber-bullying are newly coined names for what is an increasingly troubling negative consequence of living so much of our lives online, enabling those with nefarious intentions to hide behind an online presence. Being contactable 24/7 can feel intrusive. The sheer quantity of information that enters our brains isn't something our biological make-up is prepared for, and the seemingly limitless input and noise and distraction can take a toll on our cognitive functions. Walking down our streets, we're met with a sea of devices, and everyone is looking down at what's in their hands. When we're not online, we experience FOMO (fear of missing out), but what are we missing out on? That Michael likes to eat toasted teacakes for breakfast? That Jeanette has a new snazzy outfit? Algorithms help to convince us that we're missing out on the lives of other people when really, we're missing out on living our own lives. Socialising is played out through the screens of our phones and then swiftly edited and uploaded to our chosen social media platform. It's fascinating and frightening, liberating and suffocating, enlarging our world and shrinking it too.

It's important to recognise that these devices are not our enemy. Not at all; we can use our phones to order in pizza, learn about any topic, open a bank account, watch a film, read a book, track our habits, listen to a podcast or music, and sign off on a contract, all from our palm-held devices. We can create new jobs which didn't exist years ago and chat to people we've never actually met, from all corners of our globe, from wherever we are as long as we've got a reliable 4G or wi-fi connection. For those who might be isolated, social media acts as a window into the outside world; we're in control of with whom and how we connect.

It's not our actual devices which are the problem; it's how we use them.

One of the reasons these digital boundaries can be challenging to figure out is that our devices and apps come from factories and creators who've put very few boundaries, if any, in place. The crux of boundaries is that there are limits and space, around and between 'us' and everything else. With that in mind, the onus is on us to work our way through the endless settings to create boundaries which feel comfortable, safe and supportive to our health and happiness. These devices could potentially infringe on almost all areas of our lives; for example, we take a bath and take our phones with us (we even take them to the loo). They're the third wheel in our relationships, there are read receipts to contend with, and the boundaries surrounding when we can be contacted have been obliterated – that can unduly influence our mental health. These factors make navigating the relatively newly acquired and convoluted landscape of digital boundaries something we need to address – as a comparatively recent concept, we're all getting our heads around how to get them to work for us, and not against us. We're muddling along together, learning as we go.

Be Mindful of Notifications

When our devices start buzzing to alert us that our attention is demanded, we hop right to it, and when we're doing something like driving, we can't jump to it, but our focus on the task in hand is compromised. The notifications, with their vibrations, annoying tones and flashing lights, are supposed to feel 'urgent' and act as a 'call to action' to divert our attention from whatever we're doing: whether that be a message, a call, an email, a DM or a comment to reply to. Not all alerts are equal: some of these, we'll have set up mindfully so that we can be reminded to wake up at the right time, to have a drink, to take our medication and of important events.

Our phones are never very far from us; we keep them in our bags, our pockets or on the seat/table/desk next to us. Our computers have pop-ups which tell us when we have a new email, a new Slack message or a new push notification. We can, and will, be interrupted in any given moment if we have notifications enabled. Notifications mean that we have very little control over when a tug-of-war for our attention might take place. As well as the loss of control over when our focus will be interrupted, we experience a shot of cortisol when the notification sounds. Of all the times we need a shot of cortisol, it isn't when we've been tagged in a photo from a recent day out with our friends. That cortisol plays havoc with our health; from an increase in our breathing and heart rate, to sleep disruption and worst of all, a strengthening in the stress and fear memory pathways. We become primed in anticipation of receiving an alert, so much so that some of us will have experienced a phantom alert – the ones we would swear we heard/saw but when we pick up our phones, there's nothing there.

Let's not forget the added 'side' dose of cortisol that's triggered when we repeatedly switch tasks. Psychologist David Meyer has studied the effect of the toll of this constant switching back and forth between tasks, and he found that it can reduce the productivity of our brain by as much as 40 per cent![9]

Diving into the settings is a way we can regain some control, quieten our spaces and reduce levels of cortisol. We can be ultra-choosy about what we keep activated, how we're notified and when. Whilst we're at it, we can enable the blue-light filter to stop the light playing havoc with our melatonin production and take a look at any changeable settings which tell people we're online or have received/seen/read a message. Any settings edit which reduces stress, improves concentration and decreases the pressure we might feel to respond quickly is our way of drawing up the boundary drawbridge to create space for ourselves.

Consider What's Coming In...

We tend to flit from app to app when we're on our devices. A quick check-in with the news, a catch-up with what Auntie Edna is up to, a log-in to keep tabs on our bank balance, a speedy type of a reply to a comment and then we might find ourselves down a scroll-hole. We're not always mindful of when, and why, we pick up our devices, and we tend to fill holes in our day with them; the otherwise commonly occurring calm and quiet buffers of our day are now rammed with a vastness of information, and we invariably can't handle it. Our brains can't keep up, just as a computer will struggle to compute efficiently when it has too many tabs open.

---

9 Source: http://dr-hatfield.com/educ216/Multitasking%20The%20Cognitive%20Costs%20of%20Multitasking.pdf

When it comes to our social media feeds, we frequently don't exercise the power we have at our fingertips. The wading through posts that cause us to feel lacking, jaded or sub-par doesn't serve us. There's a hesitation that comes with using, at will, the options to mute, unfollow, report and block but when we mindfully curate feeds that enrich our lives with positivity, things we're interested in, motivated and inspired by, and people we genuinely like, then we feel the benefits of that from the get-go. It's a skewed sense of responsibility that comes with remaining 'friends' with those whose posts bring you down in any way, and especially to those you wouldn't speak to if you saw them walking down the street. Trust how you feel when you're scrolling; if it makes your stomach drop or triggers you to feel awful, then please do something about it. You wouldn't (hopefully) buy a magazine full of content that you felt disinterested in or disengaged and disconnected from. To some extent, we all have the opportunity to choose what we see when we log in.

...And What's Going Out

We can delete and remove posts, but basically, anything we post online acts as a digital footprint which has the potential to come back and bite us on the bum in ways we mightn't realise. If we're considering our input, it's worth being mindful of our output too; what we're sharing, where we're sharing it, why we're sharing it, who we're sharing it with – and considering if there'll be any implication in doing so that could infringe upon our privacy boundaries.

When we scroll online, we're met with intimate knowledge about those we don't know intimately. Getting acquainted is no longer an organic process, we now dive into the deep end in terms of what we know about one another.

Most recruiters and employers have access to information that they'd never have been privy to in pre-social media days. They can now actively search for social media profiles and websites of applicants and employees because our feeds tell others so much about us. The information we post online can identify where we live, who we live with, what the inside of our home looks like, the names of our pets, who we've dated, where we went to school, where we've worked and where we shop, who we're friends with, what we like to eat, drink, read, watch, listen to and do in our spare time, the politics and sports teams we support, how we speak to others, our clothing tastes and style, our preferred pronouns, our health history, our sexual orientation, the posts we've liked and shared, and so on – the list is endless – all with matching photographic entries to create a scarily accurate chronological encyclopaedia of you and those closest to you.

In 2017, a long-standing machine operator who had a clean disciplinary record was dismissed from her workplace because of a comment she wrote on Facebook. A quick google will pull up numerous results of cases where employees have had their employment terminated because of something they've published on social media.

Dating has changed completely. We can take an interest in someone, or reject them, as quickly as a swipe left or swipe right. Google will lead us down a rabbit hole of their social media profiles from which we can learn how many siblings they have, what they studied, if they know the difference between 'there' and 'their', whether they have any pets, what music they're into, whether they've had long-term partners, been married, have children, their mannerisms and all before we've given that old-fashioned thing called physical chemistry a chance!

To Share or Not to Share

It's also worth exploring the opposite side of the 'sharing' coin; the rhetoric surrounding 'oversharing', which is often met with disdain and a sneer. It's true that there are already posts aplenty which we might find loud. We might consider the space to be too overcrowded and in feeling that, we might hesitate in sharing our stories, lessons and experiences – not wanting to add to the noise, not wanting to take up space. But information is how we learn; it's how we know what we know. How we get to grips with ourselves, how we explore choices and find answers to our problems. It's not a bad thing.

As a species, it's the sharing of information that has led us to comprehend that the world isn't indeed flat, that there's this thing called gravitational pull and that most of the photographs we see in magazines are Photoshopped. This sharing also allows us to be privy to the ups and downs of life. The stigma of mental ill health is changing because people are talking about it. We're talking about stress, loneliness, burn-out, shame, guilt, money, parenting, self-care, boundaries, race and well, everything, in a raw, vulnerable and honest way.

'The stigma of mental ill health is changing.'

It broadens our horizons, our interaction with people from all walks of life and gives us insight into how people managed to do something, the challenges people are facing, the help they need, the things that have helped them, ways we can support social causes and raise social awareness. Meaningful change happens because of the sharing.

If you want to share the nitty-gritty in your corner of the internet, do. We never know who we're helping when we open that door and give those insights into how we cope, manage and live. We never know who might feel validated, seen and heard. We never know who you might be encouraging, empowering and educating.

Audit Habits

We're habitual creatures; the more regularly we do something in a certain way, the more often we'll do something in a certain way. The neural pathways strengthen, and something that may have once been alien to us becomes the norm after being repeated enough times.

How we use our smartphones, when we use them and how often we use them quite quickly becomes habitual. It's also quite a passive activity; on the face of it, it doesn't seem to require much energy or focus.

But what we see, in the rise in the number of ways we can be connected, is a disconnect with the people who matter to us. In a world where we are contactable in umpteen ways, rates of loneliness and isolation are increasing. It seems that whatever we're doing on our phones isn't meeting our needs – we're not always connecting in meaningful ways. We watch concerts through a camera screen rather than commit them to memory; meals with friends are photographed and hashtagged for Instagram; selfies show us smiling on days when we feel awful. Our camera reels are full of virtually the same photo with minor adjustments to angle, things moved out of shot and filters. In being so engaged in other people's lives, we're becoming disengaged with our own and all those in it. What we see online is an influential snapshot of a split second in time that represents a person's edited intention, opinion, thought and/or perspective.

The Power of Now

It may sound trite and clichéd but being present is the best present. And not just being present for others, being present for ourselves is essential too. We owe it to ourselves to be self-aware, tuned in and to feel as though we're the captains of our ships.

In our current climes, we're all feeling increasingly frazzled. We feel poorer, time-wise, than ever before despite the grand leaps in technology which are designed to save us time and energy. According to Ofcom's Communications Market Report, despite our perception that 'there's just not enough time in the day', the average amount of time spent online on a smartphone is 2 hours 28 minutes a day. This rises to 3 hours 14 minutes amongst 18–24s.[10] A somewhat surprising finding was that half

---

10 Source: https://www.ofcom.org.uk/__data/assets/pdf_file/0022/117256/ CMR-2018-narrative-report.pdf

of UK adults say their life would be boring if they could not access the internet.

When we feel as though there isn't enough time to do the things that we want to do, to have our needs met or to fit in all the bits and bobs that feel important to us, we can leverage our time by auditing our habits. Rather than grabbing for our phones first thing in the morning, or last thing at night, we can create a buffer to top-tail our day of non-phone time – perhaps making our bedrooms an electronic-free zone. There are apps such as AntiSocial which monitor how we use our smartphones and associated apps. They provide insights into what we do, how we do it and how much time our smartphones are eating up. We can make educated decisions based on that knowledge; to carry on happily as we were, to sometimes leave our phones in a different room, to buy a watch instead of picking up our phones to find out what time it is (often the gateway to more smartphone activity), to remove apps, to leverage that time for other interests and people.

Be Wary of Expectations

We assume that other people use their devices in the same way that we use ours. If we're super-responsive, we probably get a little frustrated when people don't reply right away – especially if we can see that the message has been received and read. If we're rarely online, the speedy replies can be a bit of a surprise.

There's a tendency sometimes to lose sight of what our smartphones are and what's going on in other people's lives. To get caught up in the micro: whether someone replied, when they were last online, whether we should nudge them to respond, and sometimes look to it as evidence that they don't like us, that we're not enough, not worthy of a response, that they're rude, getting too big for their boots, forgetting what matters, etc. etc. etc. It can really grate on us, this lack of a reply.

We've read about how slow communicating once was, and so it makes sense then, that this frantic pace might not be everyone's cup of tea. We get to choose whether we reply right away, whether we set aside a chunk of time to batch replies, how we respond, whether we uninstall an app, how often we pick up our handsets, what we focus on, whether we add/remove a connection or not, and ultimately, what's important to us and what's healthy for us. What we don't get to do is to control the actions of others by whatever means; by guilt-tripping, getting angry or using passive aggression. We must respect other people's boundaries just as we wish for ours to be respected.

We will never know what's honestly going on in another person's life. How many of these messages they receive. Whether they're burned out, on deadline, going through some pain or overwhelmed by the digital noise. Perhaps they've lost their phone, deleted the app, have forgotten to reply or are creating space for themselves. If it's someone you've never met, try to let it go. If it's someone you know in real life, then talk about it. Have a conversation about how you both manage digital boundaries and revel in the increased understanding and compassion that comes with clear communication and managed expectations.

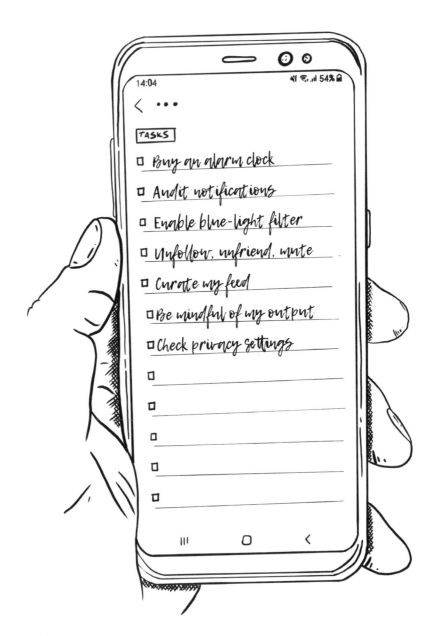

14:04   54% 🔒

<   • • •

TASKS

☐ Buy an alarm clock

☐ Audit notifications

☐ Enable blue-light filter

☐ Unfollow, unfriend, mute

☐ Curate my feed

☐ Be mindful of my output

☐ Check privacy settings

☐

☐

☐

☐

☐

Instal a social monitoring app like Antisocial.
Log the results after one week.

Are you comfortable with the results?

Yes/No

If no, how will you renegotiate time?

Create a list of self-care activities to diarise.
These will 'anchor' you.

_____

_____

_____

_____

_____

_____

_____

_____

7. Making Space in and around our work

Whatever our role at work, whether we're the new recruit, the office junior, the manager or the managing director, have worked our way up the ranks, have a zero-hour contract or a contract that requires long back-to-back shifts, workplace boundaries are challenging, and then some. Boundaries are complex things at the best of times, but workplace boundaries don't half put a cat amongst the kittens. Talking about them is like opening a can of worms and often, we feel powerless to change what's complex, ingrained, inherited and sometimes, downright unhealthy.

The term 'workplace politics' ignites a visceral reaction within us. We've all experienced a skewed power distribution at play; gossiped, been gossiped about, experienced blurred lines or confusion, trodden on toes, had our toes trodden on, felt butterflies of nerves as we've been called into a manager's office. There'll be boundaries we shouldn't have infringed upon, boundaries we rightfully challenged and boundaries of ours that just don't seem to be respected – our named food in the fridge is an example of where we try to assert our boundaries, only for them to fall on deaf ears and our food into hungry hands. That's one very simplistic instance of where boundaries are repeatedly crossed and asserting them seems fruitless because nobody seems to be listening, nor heeding. It can be demoralising.

Once upon a time, very long ago, our 'only' job was to hunt, gather and exist. As communities started forming, different skills were needed; to build shelter, tend to the sick, maintain fires, care for livestock, for example. Skills and inventions were born from a perceived need or problem – a way to streamline and make things easier, where possible. These roles became professions and the more things we invented or discovered, the more we were able to invent and discover. Each scientific leap brought with it new professions; teachers, astronomers, engineers and astronauts. There are many professions that exist today that didn't exist ten to fifteen years ago, just as there will be professions in ten to fifteen years' time which don't exist today. Advances in evolution bring with them advances in skills and needs.

If technology has disrupted the way we communicate with our friends, our family and complete strangers, then it's added another layer for consideration to the tangled web of work. With thanks to the advances in technology, we can now create businesses from our beds, manage teams from anywhere in the world and work with people we've never met in real life. We can create online shops, open bank accounts, have virtual assistants and publish our own books, podcasts and blogs. Keeping tabs or keeping in touch has never been so instantaneous with the ever-increasing number of productivity apps and integrations.

We can automate, synchronise and integrate with the click of a mouse and a few taps on our keyboard. It's never been easier to learn, carve out a career and to build, or be part of, a community of like-minded people.

Those things make boundaries blurrier than before because technology goes where we go – for so many of us, there's no escaping work, it literally follows us home.

There was also a time when our written contract was considerably more accurate in laying out the terms and conditions of our employment. There'd be exceptions, yes, but that document held weight and could be relied upon to give direction and manage expectations. We might have had to physically clock in for work and then we could also physically clock out. Working day, done. What the advent of technology has done, though, is to make it ever so tricky to eke out and protect that also-contracted non-work time. There's the written contract (hopefully!) and then we have a non-written, non-verbal, non-tangible one which encapsulates all of the added extra expectations which can't half become a burden to carry. The ever-so-casual requests for our time add up and add on to the increasing responsibility to be ultra-efficient, ultra-productive and ultra-reachable. We're answering emails late at night, working more overtime, being contacted on personal social networks, urged to feel grateful for having a job in the first place (even if it's absolutely the wrong job for us), tapping away furiously during our commutes and producing more work than we probably have been contracted for. That's all well and good if we have consciously chosen to do so but sometimes we find that we've accidentally and unconsciously made a rod for our backs.

Work boundaries can feel laden with unspoken consequences and unclear rules and limits.

If we're 100 per cent truly, honestly, comfortable with how and when we work, then there's no boundary work to be done – we get to choose what's right for us. But so many of us are experiencing stresses and strains and relationship breakdowns because of it. We worry about the ramifications if we're not checking in regularly. And let's not beat about the bush, it's well documented that some of us use work as a crutch to avoid something else that's going on in our lives – to numb feelings we'd rather not feel, pain we'd rather not experience, to avoid dealing with interpersonal situations we sense brewing. The trouble with pushing those feelings and that pain away is that they never truly go away; these things tend to pop back up in a ferocious manner when we least expect it. Using work to numb those things never tends to end well; it creates a melting pot of isolation, withdrawal from people, from experiences, from emotions, which we'll have to handle at some point.

Healthy work boundaries don't suggest that we adopt a different persona when working, and when not. Nor that we will not think about work when we're not working, or not think about personal stuff during work time: we don't have switches in our heads that help us to switch off from who we are or what we've got going on. Instead, healthy boundaries encourage us to have dedicated work time and dedicated recharging time-for-everything-else time. There should be a palpable mind shift, the lifting of the weight of workplace responsibility, and a sense that we're done for the working day. If we never feel those things, if we never get a chance to be in non-work mode, then there are some crocked boundaries to address.

Work isn't who we are. Not even if we love our jobs in an unadulterated fashion. There's more to us than that. Work boundaries help to safeguard our time, our energy, our purpose and how fulfilled we feel. Going all in leaves little for anything else. Not giving much means we always feel as though we're treading water and biding our time before we're called in for 'that' meeting. Some work boundaries are functional and clear, whilst others are more intangible and flexible. For example, we absolutely need at some point to go home and get some sleep and there are boundaries in place to ensure that happens. But when it comes to our sense of self merging with our work environment, or feeling guilty, angry or resentful, those are more fluid and sometimes less clear, more of a work in progress but no less important.

Understand Your Worth

If we never feel as though we're 'enough' we can throw ourselves into our work to try and ascertain enough-ness from our output and usefulness and indispensability. But in doing so, we tend to head towards burn-out because we move the yardstick of that enough-ness for ourselves – it'll feel further and further away the more we do, and all the while, those around us grow used to a level of output and usefulness from us. We're more likely to say yes to what's requested of us when we'd rather say no. If approval temporarily feeds our feeling enough, then that's what we'll continually seek. The trouble with that is it's dependent on how other people view us, and it isn't their approval we need but our own. The surety is that we're all enough as we are, in the here and now. We don't need to prove that to anyone, least of all to ourselves – we need to try and accept it as fact.

We're all brimming with value, even when we can't see it. The amalgamation of our experiences, our skillsets, our expertise, our energy, our insights and our perspectives has a unique value that only we have to offer – there's nobody quite like us, quirks and all. Sometimes we find ourselves in situations at work where we feel out of our depth, imposter syndrome kicks in and fear disempowers us. When really, we're there on merit, we've worked long and hard to get to where we are and those icky pains – they're growing pains. We all deserve a space at the table.

Understanding our worth and value doesn't mean we're cocky and arrogant; it's an awareness and appreciation of our achievements and of what we bring to the table, with one eye on growth and another on accepting what our weaknesses might be. It also underlines how and when we communicate, what we might be willing to do for recognition or not, what we're motivated by, how likely we are to speak up when our boundaries have been violated. When we value ourselves, our time, our energy, our skills and our expertise, we become a bit more choosy about what we take on and which balls we're quite happy to drop.

Be Clear and Concise

When we're kickstarting a conversation, one in which we would like to assert a boundary or have a defined outcome in mind, apologies can sometimes creep in: 'Sorry to bother you, but I just wanted an update on XXX.' Or, 'I hate to be a pain, but could I please chat to you about flexitime.' Being apologetic makes us sound primed for a no or for some kind of reprisal before anyone else has had any input. We feel smaller than, less important than, apologetically so. The apologies also dilute our messages so that they become unclear.

We've all had conversations where we're left not entirely sure as to what was spoken about, what is being asked of us or, even worse, as we digest what was said (or not said because our minds tend to go there) feel frustrated that we didn't speak up and out when we had the chance. We've all sent emails where we've beaten around the bush and been unnecessarily apologetic rather than just get to the point or request a phone call or meeting. How, why and when we communicate can change trajectories. When we communicate honestly and clearly, we're leaving no uncertainty behind our intention and our meaning. It opens the door for other people to do the same and means that we're not all left trying to interpret what has just been said. Confusion can, and will, crop up. Asking questions and answering questions to seek clarity is part of open and fair two-way communication. Empathy, truly listening and expressing ourselves concisely – no matter our position – creates a hotbed of confidence, trust, collaboration, innovation, change and empowered people.

It's okay to assert our boundaries. It's okay to change our minds. It's okay to share our perspectives on a situation. It's okay to be assertive and to the point. It's okay to follow up on missed deadlines, to check in and to ask for adjustments, tweaks and changes. Our contributions are valid, important and needed.

Manage and Negotiate Expectations

We start work armed with a job description and a contract of employment, a baseline set of mutual expectations; in return for doing this and that, we can expect to be remunerated in this way and that way. At the get-go, we can decline the job if we disagree with anything laid out in those baseline documents or we can negotiate. As time progresses, we might be asked to do other tasks and other projects. We might ask for workplace adjustments. The baseline evolves and that's completely natural as long as expectations remain clear, realistic and mutually agreed. They so often do not. When expectations aren't clearly defined, understood or agreed upon, it can cause a whole heap of stress for all concerned.

This is where it becomes super-important that expectations are managed, because there are often consequences which arise when expectations aren't met, and we feel the threat of those. This also applies to expectations surrounding contact outside of work hours. If there seems to be an assumed expectation, it's not unfair nor out of turn to ask for, or to create, transparent boundaries so that everyone knows where they stand. This could be a verbal discussion, in a written policy, a written agreement or setting up an email autoresponder. New expectations bring a need for differing resources: time, training, guidance, clarity, feedback loops and progress reports. The feedback loop and progress reports serve as an opportunity to raise concerns and renegotiate boundaries if needed.

Don't Get Caught Up in Gossip

A quick whisper or rant about another colleague feels harmless enough but actually, what it does is bring our integrity, credibility and trust into question. After all, if someone is talking about someone else to us, it's a fair assumption that they're likely talking to someone else about us too. When we gossip about other people, we're highlighting what we perceive to be their 'less-than' qualities – we're literally calling another's reputation into question. We're also influencing how others might view someone when really, we ought to take people as we find them, for ourselves. We're partaking in negativity for the sake of it without giving that other person the chance to have input. Gossiping is also contagious: the more it's done, the more it's done, and we underestimate the effect it has on our mood and energy and morale. Whilst it feels as though it's fostering connection, this shared highlighting of other's 'less-than-ness', can also be isolating. The forming of cliques is all well and good if you're part of the clique, but for those who aren't, it can be a pretty lonely, hurtful and distressing reality of work. In addition, nobody trusts the 'gossip'. Gossiping itself becomes a barrier to meaningful connection. It has no merits whatsoever and no place in the workplace.

Minimise Disruptions

Workplaces aren't always designed to be focus-friendly, especially open-plan offices where the hustle and bustle can be heard by all and where our desks line the walkways, open invitations for people to stop and chat as they're passing, no matter what we're doing. If we've telephones on our desks, they could ring at any given moment, a notification could ping on our computers that we've received a new email and opening an internet browser creates a whole host of possible distractions.

It's odd that more consultation hasn't been done with the people who are expected to produce good-quality work within set deadlines about what constitutes a supportive working environment – physically and mentally. Mindsets are shifting, and companies are waking up to how impactful the workplace culture and people's wellbeing is to business. But there's a mammoth way to go.

Researchers at the University of British Colombia carried out a study to see what the effects of constantly checking our emails were compared to those who checked their emails periodically throughout the day. For this study, people were asked to either check in whenever they felt like it or received a notification of a new email, or to only check their emails three times a day. For the purpose of this study, both groups received the same number of emails. Their stress levels were monitored alongside the time both groups spent on email. It's not really a surprise to learn that those who only checked in three times a day recorded lower levels of stress but interestingly, they also spent 20 per cent less time working on emails of the same volume as the other group.[11]

We can choose to be proactive in the limits we place around focused and effective work time. Where we can minimise

_____

11 Source: https://www.sciencedirect.com/science/article/pii/S0747563214005810

distractions, minimise task-switching by batching tasks of a similar nature, and allow immersion, research supports that we'll produce better quality work, feel less stressed and less overwhelmed.

Remote Working Comes with Challenges Too

It's worth considering the options available for working from home and flexi-working and questioning if no options are available and logistically could be. Perhaps we're quite introverted and working in an open-plan office is an assault on the senses. We might be a powerhouse of activity in the morning and smash through our work then, or find that the evenings are when we're more focused. Perhaps our capacity for work is determined by our health and we need the flexibility that working from home can cater to.

Working from home sounds pretty dreamy for those who've never had the opportunity. But it comes with its own unique set of boundary challenges. Things that have to be taken into consideration include: less interaction with other people can lead to isolation and loneliness, family and friends dropping by unannounced because they can, a larger requirement for self-discipline, having to create reasons to leave the house and get some fresh air, the assumption that you'll be the parent who'll take care of poorly children, knowing when to put work down when you're always at your place of work, and sometimes, the work distractions can be more plentiful as it feels less invasive to send messages/questions over a messaging app than if we had to get up and physically interrupt someone or call them. It feels easier when we can't see how busy someone is or isn't.

Working remotely requires a heightened consciousness to make space in and around work, and careful conversation and compromise to ensure those boundaries are understood and respected.

Work Out What Your Non-negotiables Are

Every decision we make is a weighing-up of the consequences and compromises. When we're asked to work overtime, there's a trade-off that occurs somewhere, with something, because we can't be in two places at once. Equally, when we're put on the spot, it can be harder to decline the requests on our time and energy. If we're not conscious of what the trade-off is, we mightn't ever have considered the things we're giving up.

Boundaries are just limits that determine what we will or won't do. Work boundaries are the parameters around what's expected of us and what we will or won't do. It's helpful to have a non-negotiables list, pre-written when we have space to weigh up the implications of the choices we make where work is concerned. If we're saying yes to overtime, what are we saying no to? Or even, what are we saying yes to? Perhaps overtime takes us away from our loved ones, but it might be that it's helping us to save for a home deposit. Perhaps our non-negotiables will be to drink a certain amount of drinks per day which then

'Boundaries are just limits that determine what we will or won't do.'

means we need to cater for that within our work schedule and factor in time to have a drink. It sounds simple, doesn't it?! But so many of us get our heads down and crush the day to find we have a headache when we leave work which could be because we're dehydrated, haven't had a break from our computer screens or a break, full stop. Non-negotiables might be that we don't ever want to miss parents' evening, a school play, taking care of our children when they're unwell. It could be that we have a reading group, a long-standing badminton game, a support group that we absolutely don't want to miss. We might not want to be contacted by work colleagues via WhatsApp, text message or social media, preferring to use those modes of communication for closest friends or family.

Creating a list of non-negotiables helps us to uncover what's important to us and then from there, we can create, communicate and negotiate boundaries to support and shield those things. When we're asked to do something, we then have a more clearly defined reasoning behind our decision-making.

Beware of Burn-out

The repercussions of mighty-merged boundaries are not just an economic cost but come with a personal cost too. We're crumbling under the pressure of being in work mode more and more and more of the time.

Whilst downtime certainly doesn't feel as productive as chasing our tails, it is productive in other ways. When we slow the tempo and rest, our brain sets to work processing all of the information, joining dots and recuperating. It's no coincidence that when we're in the shower or doing something completely unrelated to work, we have some of our best ideas – when we're relaxed, undistracted and not forcing our brain any which way. Burn-out occurs when there's an underlying expectation that is placed on us day in and day out. Quite often, it's an expectation we hold for ourselves and it is way above and beyond anything we'd expect of other people. It's that hamster-on-a-hamster-wheel steady stream of doing and delivering that causes low-level stress which catches up with us eventually. It's unsustainable and can have long-lasting repercussions for our health.

The World Health Organization has defined burn-out as 'a syndrome conceptualised as resulting from chronic workplace stress that has not been successfully managed'. It said the syndrome was characterised by: '1) feelings of energy depletion or exhaustion; 2) increased mental distance from one's job, or feelings of negativism or cynicism related to one's job; and 3) reduced professional efficacy'.[12]

We can be full-throttle passionate about our jobs; fulfilled, purposeful and motivated and still get burned out. In fact, the more passionate we might feel, the easier it is for us to justify the long hours because we take pleasure and purpose from what we're working on or towards. This is especially true for those who turn themselves inside out to serve and help others.

That drive, that tenacity, that compassion, that laser-focus is not in limitless supply, we need to harvest it. And we can do that by stepping away and creating a life outside of it which we also

---

12 Source: https://www.who.int/mental_health/evidence/burn-out/en/

derive pleasure from.

The glorification of busy isn't doing anybody any favours. It's the people who can, and do, switch off who have got it right. Not the people who burn the candle at both ends, begin and end at work, and who are always ignoring their needs to get something done. Nobody would ever pin a picture of a frazzled person on a vision board and aspire to become that. But that's who we're heading towards being if we continue to keep on keeping on with no respite, with no protective boundaries.

When we're knee-deep in the doing, it's easy to lose perspective over what's really important. When we're held to ransom over never-ending deadlines, we absolutely have to consider the long-term effects of always being 'on'. Switching off feels counter-productive, but it's playing the long game. There needs to be space between the occupancy of self and work. Taking the breaks we're entitled to is a good way to have respite and create space. That's the tea breaks, the lunch breaks, the annual leave, and if we're unwell, the sick leave. Creating space doesn't mean that we're no longer passionate, dedicated or motivated, it increases our capacity to harness more of that passion, dedication and motivation.

Some Boundaries Need to Be Challenged

When we're typically talking about boundaries it's in the context of making and holding space for others. When it comes to workplace boundaries, there's another kettle of fish to consider – the people who created the boundaries in the first place.

You see, so many of our workplace methods, systems, rules and regulations were created by the same people, for the same people. We've adopted them and we work in a way that isn't always supportive of who we are, our circumstances or where we'd like to be. Beyond a shadow of a doubt, any boundaries that perpetuate discrimination, old-fashioned rhetoric surrounding gender, basically any that negate the need for equality and equity, need to be called into account. Those archaic boundaries create unnecessary obstacles for people who want to work. They tip the scales in who we see represented in boardrooms, in our governments, on our TV screens, on the radio, anywhere and everywhere we look.

Historically, boundaries were crafted by white men, for white men, because they're the demographic which held all of the power (some would argue that's still the case). Women had to wait until 1975 (which really isn't that long ago, is it?!) before they could open a bank account solely in their name. Despite the creation of the Equality Pay (Amendment) Act in 1983 which allowed women to earn the same as men for comparable work, a report by the World Economic Forum, in 2017, believes it could take another 100 years before wage equality truly matches up.[13] When we consider how that affects the distribution of power and privilege, it's easy to see how lots of the boundaries we've inherited are tipped in favour of those who are the stereotypical 'businessman'. Which, in turn, affects the work structures we experience today.

Why is any of this a boundary issue? It means that depending

---

13 Source: https://www3.weforum.org/docs/WEF_GGR_2017.pdf/

on your demographic, particularly for marginalised groups, the opportunities available aren't on an equal footing. And they should be, for everyone. There's a distribution of power which is taking aeons to challenge and change and that's because the boundaries in place serve the people who have the power to change them the most.

It takes an immense amount of courage to challenge the status quo, to speak up when things don't feel right, to instigate meaningful change. But change is happening, however painfully slowly that may be. Both France and Germany have created laws which legally provide employees with the 'right to disconnect', and people like Anna Whitehouse, aka Mother Pukka, are campaigning tirelessly on behalf of us all for the right to work flexibly; not just parents, everyone.

Lead the Way

If we're the leaders at work, then boundaries can be particularly onerous. Knowing the buck stops at you can be a weighty obligation, one that's a conduit to sleepless nights, worry and self-doubt. The juggling of the strategies, cash flow, endless decision-making and taking care of a team, means that it can be difficult to focus – who knows when the next 'quandary' might occur and demand our attention. That in and of itself can cause anxiety; always being primed and ready to problem-solve can mean that we're constantly on high alert.

There's a difficulty too that comes with being present in the here and now. As leaders, we need to have the ability to reflect

'Energy management is crucial; making room for the ebbs so that the rest can flow.'

and analyse and learn from what's gone by. Concurrently, we need to have the ability to look ahead, plan, foresee obstacles and forecast. People skills are needed too; to nurture, navigate tricky situations, help people play to their strengths, knowing when to encourage and when to sit in the darkness with someone, as well leading by example where self-care is concerned. Hats, so many different hats that we wear.

We don't always consider how much a leader gives of themselves nor what it takes to balance all of the aspects of their role. Energy management is crucial; making room for the ebbs so that the rest can flow. Allowing space for a team to develop, grow and make mistakes is important for autonomy and limiting the day-to-day decision-making. Knowing when enough is enough when it comes down to working with people who may be rude, constantly disrespectful of boundaries, and make unreasonable demands, and then having the courage to follow through with the consequences of that.

On top of it all, a leader really influences how a team feels; supported, heard, held, part of something, valued, energised. There are leaders who inspire and those who make us feel small, irrelevant, replaceable. There are bosses who rule with an iron rod and those who fully embrace listening to the insights of the team and making space for those insights to shape future projects or trajectory. Workplaces can be supportive or constrictive and it'll be largely down to the person who is leading the way.

Work boundary check-in

Time to have awareness and appreciation of your achievements. List 'em!

 # My non-negotiables

- _____

- _____

- _____

- _____

- _____

- _____

- _____

- _____

8. Making Space: culturally, societally and environmentally

Our cultures, societies and environments are nuanced, dynamic, complex and laden with expectations, codes of conduct, beliefs, and frameworks within which we live and behave and interact with the world around us and the people within it. Much of this we inherit from the generation that's been before us, through their teaching and our imitating. It's something we often adopt without question.

Culturally, there are many factors within which we diversify; our heritage, economics, language, education, customs, behaviours, politics, resources, geography, beliefs, class, age, abilities, values, food, music and art, clothing, family, sexual orientation, religious and spiritual beliefs. All of those cultural factors provide a divergent set of experiences, perspectives and insights which are impossible to assign a generalised label to. They provide unspoken rules which guide the way we live and yet, we can experience cultural shifts as we evolve, individually and collectively.

Societies and cultures are different things. Societies are organised groups of people who operate in an ordered way: a given society is the sum of its members. It's the coming together of people who reside in the same place geographically and who share similar cultures and behaviours, from which societies are formed. The structure, legal rules and systems – what's considered illegal and legal – within a society are influenced by its culture but those constructs can pressure a culture, socially, to behave in line with societal expectations. Within society, we can often feel stereotyped, as though we've been labelled one way or another. But culturally, we've shown how difficult that is to do.

The environment around us pertains to anything that surrounds us and influences us; physically, biologically, socially and mentally. Our physical environment tends to be our homes, our belongings, the landscape, our geographical placement, the planet and solar system, and how the climate affects us. Our biological environment includes all living things; people, animals and plants. Our social environment includes the cultures, the economics, the education and the institutions. Our mental environment is the impact of the physical, biological and social environments upon our mental health.

Once we've worked on the boundaries within ourselves, our interpersonal relationships and the things immediately surrounding us, we can extend that to how our actions and behaviours might impact and influence our culture, society and environments. Nothing in life is certain, that's the only thing we can be certain of. We never know what's on the horizon that

> *'Nothing in life is certain, that's the only thing we can be certain of.'*

might cause a U-turn in our circumstances. There might come a time when we find ourselves fighting for equality and equity.

Equality is the notion of fairness for all, to ensure people are not discriminated against, treated differently, or unfairly, for any reason, consciously or sub-consciously – no matter who they are. It doesn't level out the playing field as we often assume it does. Imagine schooling. Equality would have us teaching all children in exactly the same style, equally distributing attention and resources, and then expecting equal outcomes from those children.

What that doesn't address though, is equity. When working towards a more balanced society, it's equity that we really need to look at. Equity is when resources and policies deliberately favour those who typically experience discrimination to create a more likely chance of catching up and of opportunity. If we take a look back at our schooling example, equity would be ensuring that all children can access schooling, adapting learning styles, distributing more attention and resources to those who aren't on a level playing field with the rest of the class. It's about giving more to those who have less and actively working to stop the historical oppression of groups of people.

At the moment, the world currently feels pretty divided and hostile because it is. Decades of work towards equity is being undone by the overturning of laws and fostering of hate by those in power. It's frightening and it all feels increasingly uncertain, unsettling and frightening. There's an ever-increasing amount of people who are creating fortress boundaries surrounding the news because it feels like self-care to do so – they're muting, blocking and disengaging. The pictures of war-torn countries, dying children, abortion being made illegal, desperate refugees, knife crime, hate rising are bound to have an impact and they do. Whether that's to incite anger, despair, hopelessness or helplessness, we'd have to be robots to not feel something. It feels easier to ban it all from our day-to-day to protect ourselves from those feelings.

It's pretty impossible to fully shun it all though; there's a palpable sense of what's happening, we can kind of feel it in the way we're interacting with others, with an increasing number of protests, with the backtracking of laws and the rise in anger. It's hard to ignore, no matter how much we evade, mute and disengage. That limbo between wanting to protect ourselves, but existing within an atmosphere of discontentment, change and injustice can cause a low-level but never-quite-going-away rumble of cultural, societal and environmental anxiety.

No news doesn't equate to good news, it narrows our perception on what's really going on and leaves our brain to join the nefarious dots. It sucks us into a fake vacuum where life as we know it is hunky-dory yet in our peripheral vision there are millions of people living through hell.

How is any of this a boundaries thing? Part of boundary work is understanding that we are responsible for our action (or inaction). It's understanding the impact our choices have on our environments and making

'No news doesn't equate to good news.'

well-balanced decisions upon that understanding. Understanding that if we carry on as we have been doing with consumption and waste, our legacy for the generations to come is an inhospitable planet. In valuing the freedom we have, it's not a stretch to imagine how awful life must be for those who are oppressed. If we were in any way disadvantaged, discriminated against, or in danger's way, we'd be completely reliant on the help, support and action of people just like us.

'The very act of partaking in self-care is an act of rebellion.'

Start Where You Are

We're all carrying burdens; whether that be ill health, trying to make ends meet, ending toxic relationships, dealing with bullying, whatever it might be – life isn't ever plain sailing, it can be (and often is) downright tricky. If we're running on empty with nothing left to give, then that's our first and foremost cause to tackle; topping up that energetic, emotional, health deficit. It's become a cliché but it's true, we really can't pour from an empty cup – trying to do so leads us down the not-so-merry path of resentment, burn-out and ill health. We can't give what we don't have to give.

Self-care is a healthcare issue. It's preventative, transformative and makes space for us to take what we *need* mentally, emotionally, physically, energetically and spiritually. It helps us to be self-aware and mindful of our thoughts, choices and actions, constantly and continually. The very act of partaking in self-care is an act of rebellion and sends a signal to those around us that it's okay to do the same, a lovely ripple effect.

So many of us keep on keeping on, ignoring our internal cues to stop, to take stock and to recharge. When life feels as though it's bursting at the seams and everything feels hard – even the most intuitive and seemingly simple of tasks – then that's a massive internal neon sign equivalent saying 'stop!'. We all know how this feels; a weariness that sleep doesn't seem to shift, clumsiness, forgetfulness, heavy bones, foggy head, aches and pains, numbness, apathy, lots of emotions bubbling up, wired and tired at bedtime, a slowing down of our cognitive functions, relationships feeling harder, crankiness, emotional shutdown, no energy to brush our teeth or deal with life admin.

If we're starting where we are and we're currently feeling any of those things, then yes, it's absolutely time to pull up the drawbridge for a spell, to construct robust boundaries to make room for recovery; prioritise and renegotiate expectations, cancel what we can, ask for help, say 'no' to anything that doesn't light us up and build in pauses. Doing nothing is never doing nothing, it's resting, recharging, recuperating, making space.

Question Everything

Our brain functions in such a way that it seeks patterns, seeks out what it knows and seeks out those who are similar to us – it always wants us to take the easy route. That's why change can feel so difficult, it literally conflicts with how our brain prefers to work. And, let's face it, nobody enjoys feeling conflicted.

There's an old story about how a lady would lop off the end of a joint of meat before she placed it in the cooker. Somebody asked her why and she explained she did it because her mum had done it. Being asked 'why' made her wonder why her mum had done it and so she asked her mum the same question. Funnily enough, her mum had the same answer: she did it because her mum always had. Again, being asked 'why' got her thinking and so she asked her mum why she always cut the end off before cooking. Her mum responded 'Because our oven was so small, we couldn't fit the whole joint in, I always had to cut the end off.'

How many things do we do, think, believe or say, because we're simply modelling behaviours we saw growing up? Some of the behaviours we've adopted won't necessarily serve us, but we do them because we always have, because someone before us always did. It's healthy to question everything, including ourselves. To stay curious, to understand why we do the things we do. To question some of the rules we might abide by that don't at all align with who we are. To evaluate if any of the rules or systems hold us back, limit us, confine us and do away with the ones which do. There are boundaries we'll end up keeping, some we'll end being more flexible about and those we'll do away with altogether once we get gritty about the whys, wheres, whats, hows and whens.

You Can Play a Vital Role in Meaningful Change

You absolutely can. Swap your plastic-wrapped toilet rolls for the eco-friendly ones from Don't Give a Crap who donate 50 per cent of their profits to help build toilets and improve sanitation in the developing world. Buy your organic, free-from-toxins tampons from Ohne who donate to a 'Girls Programme' in rural Zambia which provides innovative health education, improves hygiene through the building of new and clean toilet blocks, and helps girls learn how to make reusable pads and learn to sew. Buy an extra packet of pasta when shopping and pop it in the local food-bank collection box near the checkout. Donate any unwanted unopened items using DropPoint, a website that directs you to charities and non-profit organisations that would benefit from the goods you want to give away. There are an increasing amount of social enterprises and initiatives which replace supermarket items with products that are kinder to cultures, societies and the environment.

It's also never been easier to find like-minded people to unite over a shared passion for things to change, for our awareness to widen and our actions to have impact. Our impact is often greater than we understand and realise it to be. Passion, integrity and determination are infectious. When we talk with our peers about environmental, cultural and societal issues, we increase awareness and understanding which ripples out through families and friends. Lots of us went to school where they didn't teach this stuff and so we're having to teeter into the unknown and shut down that feeling of ignorance and clumsiness that comes from a place of privilege.

We can leave people, and the planet, better than we found them. And we do that by caring. Caring about equality and equity. Considering our carbon footprints, how much waste we create, speaking up and speaking out. We can volunteer, highlight matters, lobby, protect, campaign, donate, fundraise and sign petitions. We can work together to build bridges and smash those barriers and glass ceilings which try to belittle and undermine our confidence. The ones which protect the wrong people and create widespread vulnerabilities. We can rally our peer-troops into action to help create boundaries to keep us, and others, from harm.

If We're Ever Stuck for Ideas ...

When we look for them, we can see examples of everyday people doing extraordinary things. Whether it's your mate Gary climbing a mountain for a charitable cause, your cousin Debra who set up a local support group, or the hundreds and thousands of people who volunteer their time in soup kitchens, for the Samaritans and for a whole host of social causes. There really is a way we can all contribute our resources, in some capacity.

Social media gives us a gateway to hate and division, but it also provides access to people, just like you and me, who are banging the drum, marching to their own beat and slaying the floor with the reality of how lives are for other people. It affords the chance to widen our knowledge and awareness, to stop operating in a vacuum and to open our eyes. It can be powerful, liberating and change-making.

Here are just a few examples of incredible everyday people who are standing up, loudly, proudly and resoundingly, for what they believe in:

Greta Thunberg

Twelve years. Twelve short years is the timeframe we've been given by the Intergovernmental Panel on Climate Change within which we need to reduce our CO_2 emissions by 50 per cent and make considerable changes to our existing systems to prevent the irreversible trajectory that we're heading towards.

Activist Greta Thunberg has been shining the spotlight on climate change by urging us to understand that our 'house' – the planet – is on fire. And just as we'd panic and take immediate action if the roof over our head was on fire, she's encouraging us to panic and take immediate action to alter the course our planet is on. Aged sixteen, she's spoken at the World Economic Forum, to MPs in parliaments across the world, masses of media outlets and inspired hundreds of thousands of young people to protest. If you ever doubt whether one person can evoke change, here's the evidence to show that one person can do just that.

Candice Braithwaite

I met Candice as we were both on Team Bangs on the Run and ran a half marathon together. I was struck then by how beautiful her brain was and how she could sum up thoughts and feelings in a really captivating and eloquent way. You kind of want to hang on her every word and soak up all the wisdom and truthbombs which fall from her lips.

Since then, Candice has been using her voice to challenge the diversity we see on social media and in campaigns in the media, particularly when it comes to motherhood, with Make Motherhood Diverse. It's a campaign which gives under-represented mothers the opportunity to speak about their experiences using the pictures and words of their choosing. Their aim is to represent every experience equally, democratically and inclusively.

Gina Martin

We've seen such pictures plastered across magazines, but how would you feel if someone took a photo of your nether regions? It's called upskirting and until recently there were no laws to protect us from this grotesque sexual act which has been reported to have happened to children as young as ten years old.

Thank goodness for Gina Martin. Gina was at a festival when she caught a man looking at a photo of someone's crotch. From what she was wearing, she knew it was a photo of her that had been taken without her consent. Understandably distressed and angry, Gina took his phone from him and told a security guard who subsequently rang the police. Other than tell the man to delete the photo, the police explained that there was nothing that could be done – it wasn't, at that time, a criminal offence to take a sexually intrusive photo. What followed was a viral Facebook post, a petition which received 50,000 signatures within days and a tireless eighteen-month campaign to criminalise the act. Upskirting is now a sexual offence in England and Wales, punishable by up to two years in prison.

Martin Lewis

You might recognise Martin Lewis from the telly, he's frequently on our screens advising us about our financial rights and is the man behind the useful website Money Saving Expert. What you mightn't know is that Martin founded the charity Money and Mental Health, which works to break the link between financial difficulty and mental health problems. The website **www.moneyandmentalhealth.org** has such a wealth of information and Martin and his team campaign relentlessly for changes in the financial services industry, in regulation, national policy and in the health system.

In June of 2019, the UK government announced its plans for Breathing Space, a debt respite scheme which will protect those in problem debt from debt enforcement action, including people experiencing a mental health crisis. This plan was a direct result of a Money and Mental Health campaign and will dramatically change the lives of those who are mentally unwell.

Alexandria Ocasio-Cortez

When it comes to politics, we often feel unrepresented and powerless. We mightn't think our vote matters but when it comes to elections, a huge amount of people don't vote – enough to totally sway the outcomes.

Alexandria Ocasio-Cortez (AOC) is a shining beacon of an example of how grassroot communities can influence the political landscape. AOC is the congresswoman from New York's 14th district, and her campaign was largely funded by grassroot donations with an average of $22. From the off, it didn't seem likely that she'd win the primary, but she did and went on to become the youngest woman to ever serve the United States Congress.

When it comes to advocating, it's for progression: Medicare for all, free public college and trade school, a 70 per cent marginal tax rate for incomes above $10 million and constantly challenging the motivations of politicians who have been backed by corporate funding. What's so impactful, too, is that AOC talks about politics and policies in layman's terms, furthering access to and education about politics. She's an absolute delight on social media too.

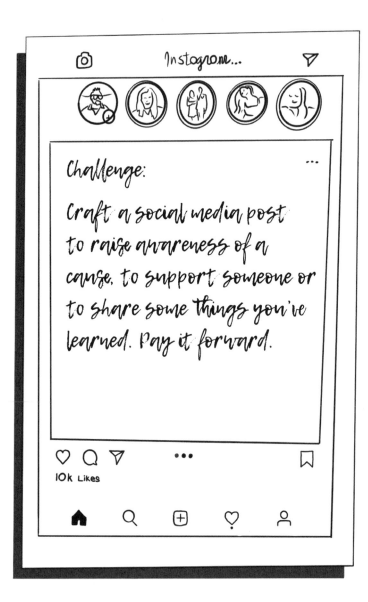

Write a letter from future-you to now-you.

Meaningful change pledge

I pledge to:

_____

_____

_____

_____

9. Emergency boundaries

There are times when we feel as though we're backed into a corner and we need an action plan, pronto. Here are some boundary-related actions for those boundary-related 'Argh, I can't think' times.

Ways to Say 'No'

'No' *is* a complete sentence but sometimes it doesn't feel emphatic enough, and other times it feels too blunt. Here are some alternative ways to express your 'no'. You might feel awkward doing so, but a good exercise is to repeat these aloud in front of a mirror so that you can get used to saying the words and not feel so awkward when the opportunity presents itself to assert your 'no'.

Not on your nelly
No way
That's not going to happen

You've got another think coming
N to the O, no
Heck, no
Not in a million years
It's a no from me
No can do
I'm sorry, but I can't
That's not going to work for me
I'm not taking on any more commitments at the moment
I've a bit much on my plate right now
Perhaps next time, when things have quietened down for me
I'm not currently in a position to help with this
Gah, I'm tied up with something else then
I'm making an effort to not overcommit myself like I have in the past, so it's a no this time
I'm going to pass on this
Thank you for thinking of me, but it's not something I've capacity for
I can't help with this, but I can put you in touch with someone who might be able to
I'd have loved to, but my schedule is looking pretty crammed at the moment
Everything's feeling a little messy for me right now so I'm in a 'subtracting' not 'adding' stage
I'm going to have to pass on this occasion, but please bear me in mind for next time

What to Do When You're at the End of Your Tether

Our tolerance is changeable because it's dependent on so many factors. We might feel pushed to the end of our tether by something one day which, on any other day, would have been water off a duck's back. Or perhaps we've the patience of a saint and we've put up and shut up for longer than has been healthy for us. Being at the end of our tether is especially difficult if communication isn't our strong point and also because, when we're there, all kinds of emotions can bubble up – momentarily clouding our judgement.

1 ASK FOR HELP

If life's problems have built up and are swamping you, please ask for help. If it's not forthcoming the first time, you're worth asking for it again. You deserve the help and support you need. It's horrible being in a position of needing help, but we've *all* been there. It feels vulnerable, weak and hopeless but asking for help is an act of hope, courage and strength because it takes us from that disempowered and helpless state to one of empowerment and help.

2 MAKE SPACE

It's hard to see any other perspective when we feel floored. Especially if we're experiencing a cocktail of emotions, are feeling afraid, lost, betrayed, empty and crumbled. Make space for the emotions to settle, take yourself away from the situation if you can, and express the stress – journal, rant, offload, cry, etc. Often when we give ourselves that space, we're able to weigh up the situation a bit more rationally and a solution presents itself.

3 SELF-CARE

Slowing down when we feel so up against it feels counterintuitive but that's the exact time when we need to pull out the soothing tools which have helped us so many times before. Self-care also includes things like dealing with a creditor who is chasing for money rather than burying our heads in the sand. Perhaps it's making that health appointment we've been putting off which could give us peace of mind or at the very least, give us answers so we know where we stand. Perhaps there's an icky conversation we've been procrastinating about, which could really take the weight off our shoulders. Whatever future-you would thank now-you for is self-care.

4 FOLLOW THROUGH

Relationships are tough. The coming together with another person who is bringing their own unique experiences, perspectives, assumptions and baggage, and trying to forge a connection takes effort, compassion and patience. But there are occasions when our boundaries are dishonoured, time and time and time again. When that happens, we absolutely have to be willing to follow through on the (often threatened) consequences of our boundary infringements. We can't keep compromising ourselves for someone who is being so uncompromising. Boundaries are the crux of healthy relationships.

You've Made a Mistake, or Ten

There is no such thing as a mistake-less life, there honestly isn't. We all make mistakes, we just don't like to draw attention to them and announce them on a Tannoy for the world to hear. We typically fret around trying to cover our tracks and to appear as though we have all our shizz together. And that's what we're faced with when we log into any social network: a wall of people looking as though they have their ducks in a row. It's a façade. Mistakes are part and parcel of life. It's how we handle the aftermath which determines whether we'll grow through what we go through or be felled by it.

1 RE-FRAME THEM

The word 'mistake' comes with all of the 'whoopsy-daisy's, 'oh no's and 'gah, how could I be so stupid?'s that themselves come from a place of guilt, shame and vulnerability. We only know what we know. Mistakes are born from a lack of knowledge, experience and sleep – yup, it's hard to weigh up things cognitively when our cognitive functions are weary. If we can only look at mistakes as lessons, then it becomes all the more interesting. Lessons teach us things, they're valuable, they help us to stay curious, they equip us with what it was that we didn't know in the first place. When it comes down to it, all mistakes are lessons, that's all they are. Even the painful humdingers teach us something. Look for the lessons.

2 BE KIND TO YOURSELF

When our children or friends make mistakes, we're the first to swoop in with soothing words of kindness and compassion. What we don't do is chuck criticism, nastiness and told-you-sos at their already bruised souls. Nothing can bloom from a tirade of insults. Creating a toxic dialogue doesn't serve us in any which way. You can make mistakes and still be a kind person. Nobody is infallible, nobody. Speak to yourself as you would your children or a friend – you deserve your own kindness, even when you've messed up.

3 MOST THINGS ARE SORT-OUT-ABLE

In the aftermath of a mistake-fest, everything feels broken. We might feel broken by it, relationships might feel broken by it, people around us might feel shaken by it and life how we saw it now looks so different. The thing to remember is that everything we feel and experience is temporary. The sun will shine again, and the darkness will fade. It will. Most things are sort-out-able, even when we can't see the solution. Give yourself time to deal with the aftershock and then, when you feel calmer and time has healed you, start to take action to learn, make amends, communicate, reflect and strive to not make the same mistake twice.

Nobody Seems to Be Listening

This boundary malarkey is difficult, there's no bones about it. It's a constant kerfuffle of learning, asserting, flexing, reflecting, communicating and questioning. When we feel as though nobody is listening or heeding our boundaries, it can make us feel less than, diminished, unseen, misunderstood and unimportant.

1 **BE CLEAR**
When we make a foray into this boundary stuff, we can wobble about quite a bit because it's all so new. It's very much like a child learning to walk; they teeter, fall down and get up again, until one day they're walking briskly and confidently, like never before. Boundary work is a skill, it's a habit we can learn and unlearn. We can know something to be true and right for ourselves because we feel it to our core, but communicating those things is often what upsets the apple cart. When we're talking to other people about our boundaries we need to be clear, because being clear is being fair. It negates ambiguity and crossed wires. When we apologetically assert ourselves, it fogs up our messaging and topples the distribution of power. In apologetically expressing our boundaries, it's as if we're expecting and anticipating them not being heard, heeded or respected.

2 BE ALIGNED

The people who are least likely to listen are those who were served the most by us having such wonky boundaries. Why would they want things to change, right? They loved things just as they were. But you didn't love things the way they were, which is why you're here, and that balance needs redressing. Our words have such power but, by golly, that power is magnified when our actions align with them. Clearly communicating our boundaries is a scary first step, but aligning our actions with them is when they become turbocharged. If we're sending out mixed messages, we can understand why there may be confusion; if what we're saying and what we're doing don't match up and make any sense, we can see why people may have tuned out. Stay clear, consistent and keep your actions aligned with your words.

3 IS IT A GOOD TIME?

Once we've decided we want to talk about something important, we often have an expectation that those around us should sit up and listen on demand. There are so many reasons as to why that mightn't happen; they might have had a terrible day, they could be in the middle of something that requires their undivided attention, and so on. Approaching the conversation with 'I'd like to talk to you about something, is now a good time?' means you're respecting their boundaries of time, energy and needs, as well as bringing up the fact you would like to talk. If now is a good time, great, dive in. If it's not, ask when would be a good time and try again then.

4 WRITE A LETTER

The truth can hurt and when we're having these loaded conversations, they can be stacked with hurts of old. So much of our communication is non-verbal, which can make these conversations all the trickier because of what our faces, our posture, our reactions can convey. When we write down what we want to say in a letter, it strips back the defences and the offences, and gives us the opportunity to lay it all bare. We tend to be more compassionate this way too, as we've space to really consider our words and their impact. When it feels as though nobody is listening, writing a letter could be the start of a bridge being built.

5 LISTEN TO YOURSELF

When we don't feel listened to, it can seem as though we're shouting into the abyss, hoping that someone will care, and it's a horrible feeling. One thing that we can do that's quite practical is to make sure that we are 100 per cent truly tuning in and listening to ourselves. So often we're not. If we're super-clear on who we are, our needs, wants, dreams and goals, then our actions will follow suit. We only become super-clear on those things by tuning in and listening to our gut, our envy, to our visceral reactions and to how things make us feel. If we're listening, if we care, if we're taking responsibility to ensure that our needs, wants, dreams and goals are met, then anyone listening outside of that is secondary and suddenly, it's less important that they do so.

6 **FIND YOUR PEOPLE**
We might outgrow relationships and sometimes they outgrow us. When that happens, we can feel unanchored and all at sea. Look to build a community for yourself. Whether that be joining a running club, a craft workshop, a book club, a closed Facebook group, looking for a meet-up, a mastermind or local events. Surround yourself with people who are on your wavelength instead of adjusting your wavelength, minimising your light and compromising who you are to keep relationships going well past what's healthy and meaningful. It's not just you who deserves better, the other person in the relationship deserves better too.

Surrounded by Barricades

We only build barricades from a place of fear, pain and hurt because we think they'll keep us safe. If we glance back into our past, the reasons are often there, glowing like beacons to validate why they are needed. The trouble with barricades is that they block out everything: the good, the beautiful, the bad and the downright nasty. When our defences are impenetrable, they can feel like a prison. It's an all-in or all-out approach which exists in a black and white world, but we know that the world exists in a gazillion shades of grey. With an epidemic, too, of loneliness, learning how to convert those barricades to boundaries is safer for our overall health then being isolated and disconnected.

1 ALLOW YOURSELF TO FEEL AND HEAL

Suppressing our feelings over and over stunts our growth and keeps us stuck. The knock-on effect is that we often take responsibility for things outside of our remit, we have low self-esteem, low self-worth and a lack of self-trust and trust in others. What's worse is that these unexpressed and undealt with feelings become limits we place on ourselves. If we're not allowing some feelings through, then feelings of joy and happiness will also struggle to get through. Book into counselling, speak with friends, journal, dance (motion and emotion have an interesting connection) and be mindful of how you speak to yourself. Self-kindness is transformative.

2 VOLUNTEER

When we pull up the drawbridge and prevent anything or anyone that's kind, caring, been there, from coming in, it's usually because we're being eaten up by shame or by fear for our emotional and mental safety. We've nothing to be ashamed of, nothing; even when that shame brings tears to our eyes and makes our hearts race with panic, we've nothing to be ashamed of. Shame is one of the heaviest burdens we can carry but we don't have to punish ourselves by carrying it around any longer. Talking about shame is a sure-fire way to expel it, and one of the ways we can do that is to volunteer our time to help other people who may be in the same boat. There's solidarity in finding people with shared experiences, there's a certain therapeutic element to using our painful experiences to ease the suffering of others, and there's a connection that comes with the 'knowing nod' that is like a warm and gentle hug for the heart.

3 NEW CHAPTERS

How we feel about ourselves doesn't half get skewed when life gets skewed. It's hard not to let our past become part of our identity as we're shaped and moulded by our experiences. How we see the world changes each day, based on what that day held. The extremes – the really truly great stuff and the flippin' awful, terrible stuff – shape us more than anything else could. The thing with carrying all of that baggage and living behind a barricade is that it's as if our wings have been clipped. Try not to let the past dictate the future or crush the vastness of untapped potential. The past is a chapter in your story, but it's not the start, middle and end of who you are, and who you could be. You get to write new chapters as you go. You're also worth more. You're worth connection, happiness, love, laughter, good things, good times and those dreams of yours.

4 YOU HAVE A SUPERPOWER

We all have a superpower that's unique to us. It's the natural gift we have to give to the world. Bad times sometimes blind us to our value, our strengths and our power, but it's there, nonetheless. If we have people around us who we trust to ask, we could send them a text and ask 'What are my strengths? What are my best bits? What's my superpower?'

Done People-pleasing

This is a somewhat confusing spiderweb of boundary infringing because it sees us taking on so much responsibility that's not ours to take on under the guise that we've got love, commitment and kindness at our core. The boundaries being crumpled are two-way, too: ours and theirs.

1 **THE FEARS**
Prolific people-pleasers tend to have fears of abandonment, of being rejected, of whether they're liked and of whether they're enough. From there we try and make ourselves indispensable, useful and of value to everyone and their dog. It's a sure-fire way to wrap ourselves up in knots, to deplete our energy reserves and to do away with boundaries altogether. We're worthy, important and valuable as people, just because. We don't actually have to do anything for that to be true because it's true for us all from the moment we are born.

2 **HONOUR YOURSELF**
If we would go to the moon and back to avoid conflict, to avoid criticism, to avoid being disliked, then you can bet your nelly that we're not feeling our own power. In fact, the power scales are so tipped out of our favour that we have no expectations of ourselves past the fact that we'll do anything we can to meet the ever-increasing expectations of others. We're dancing to their tune, their drumbeat, and we're wondering why we're so utterly exhausted.

Honour your emotional and energetic limits, don't give what you don't have to give, value your resources, make time for you, listen to your needs and take responsibility for those being met, set clear and healthy boundaries, don't get sucked into gossip, criticism and judgement, think of yourself as an equal and don't take it personally if someone doesn't accept your offer of help.

3 STOP APOLOGISING

In apologising for everything, we almost end up apologising for our very existence. It's okay to express our feelings and opinions, it's okay to not be okay, it's okay to make mistakes, it's okay to root for yourself and it's okay to say no to the things you don't have the energy, passion, time or heart for. The things we absolutely do not have to apologise for: when someone knocks into us, for speaking up and speaking out, for any of our feelings, for having needs, for taking time away, for the anger of others, for other people's actions, for being different, for choosing you.

4 RESPONSIBILITY CHECK

It's not always obvious but taking responsibility for others is a downright infringement of their boundaries. In swooping in to mend, fix, eliminate unease, iron out their feelings, to dish out unsolicited advice, speak on their behalf, we're crossing the line between their identity and ours, between what's our responsibility and what's not. We're not allowing them to learn from their mistakes, to stand on their own two feet; we're not giving them the space to reflect on what they need, to feel a sense of achievement when they've found a solution or overcome an obstacle off their own steam; and sometimes, we're putting words into their mouths. The things we're not responsible for: meeting other people's needs, their actions, their choices, reading their minds, fixing their problems, their happiness, their anger, their sadness, their hurdles, their opinion of us, their finances... the list truly goes on and on.

5 ACCEPT HELP

People-pleasers aplenty will find this one incredibly difficult. When we're used to being the helper, it can totally lead us to doubt the intentions of others when we're in need of help (because our intentions aren't always as selfless as they seem on the surface). It's just not something we're used to. We close ourselves off to the help we need because from the get-go we worry about how we'll ever repay it, what we can do to even the 'score', and we feel innately that we're entirely undeserving. Accept help when it's offered, get used to taking as well as giving, express your gratitude and try to remember that most people love to help without caveats, without expecting anything in return.

A letter from me to you

Hey you,

You may well have read this book and been nodding your head because you have totally got this boundary stuff nailed. If that's the case, all the well dones, I wish I'd met you years ago, you boundary-magic-maestro you. Give yourself the biggest of pats on the back, bask in being a boundary oracle and then pass this book to someone who might need a little help.

You may well have read this book and had head-nods of a different kind; those ever-so-painful face-slaps of realisation that perhaps there's some work for you to do. If you've unearthed some uncomfortable truths and evoked emotions you didn't even realise were buried inside you, please know this: it's not your fault, nope. Up until now, it's not been your fault. If you didn't know, you didn't know, so please don't let the growing pains cause you to switch into self-criticism mode. Make space for the dust to settle, for reflection and for some comforting and reassuring self-care – that's boundary work in and of itself.

Once our eyes are open to something, it's really hard to close them again. Once you've learned about boundaries, you can't ever unknow it. It will feel as though you're being served boundary test after boundary test once you have read this book, and you'll be hyperaware of your thoughts, words and actions, and those of others. It can feel like opening a can of worms, as though life has turned up the stress dial, but it hasn't – your tolerance to the drama, to the stressors, to the people who try to overpower you, has reduced, and that's a very, very good thing. You'll be able to plainly see and feel when boundaries are wonky-tonk as though you're holding a magnifying glass up to your interactions with everything and everyone else.

Work through the bits that cause any kind of friction or contradiction for you, bit by bit, slowly but surely. Revisit the worksheets, have those conversations you've been putting off, call in the troops for support, embrace your you-ness, and see those efforts as giving yourself the biggest gift of all – a life that fulfils, inspires and makes you smile. It's the very least you deserve. Honestly, you do deserve to be happy. Yes, you. Yes, you do.

If, up to now, the self-chatter has been pretty grotty and critical, tweak your actions to align with who you want to be and what you want to do and keep plugging away at that. Create an environment for yourself that supports, nurtures and provides space for you to grow. Prove those fearful thoughts wrong: you can, and you will. In wanting to be kind and giving, always ask yourself, 'Is this kind for me too?'

Choosing yourself feels selfish but it's anything but. The people who truly love us and want the best for us don't want to see us on our knees, depleted, unhappy and broken. They truly don't. There's a barometer in there somewhere too, for it separates the wheat from the chaff, this boundary stuff. And that is not a reflection on you, nope, no siree. It's a truth that has been there all *along but covered up with the bending backwards, side-stepping, over-accommodating and compromising of ourselves.*

Those people who we no longer serve with our brand-spanking-new boundaries won't be happy about it, because things were perfect for them just as they were. But for you, they can't have been, because you were drawn to a book about boundaries – you knew on some level that things were awry. Go easy on yourself, don't shoulder the upset or carry the burdens of another's disappointment, it's not yours to carry.

Always learning with you and rooting for you, you've so got this.

Jayne x

These are a few of my favourite things

As I evolve and grow and learn, so too, do the things I find useful, helpful, motivating, inspiring and interesting. I'm extremely mindful of what I might be met with when I open up social media apps and of how I want to feel when I do so. Decluttering the apps on my phone is also something I do regularly because I want to get the best out of my phone, not for the phone to get the best out of me.

Here's a list of websites, social media accounts and apps that's I'm loving right now.

www.blurtitout.org
No surprises that our website has top spot! I genuinely find the content valuable and there's a certain sense of therapy that's come from taking the tough periods in my life and turning them on their head into something meaningful. Most recently we ran a Crowdfunder (massive thank yous to all who supported it) and the comments blew me, and the team I work with, away. We're making a difference and that's a mighty fine thing to know.

Flipd

This app is the ultimate phone boundary for those of us who are sick and tired of falling down scroll-holes. Flipd will, on schedule if you choose, completely block your phone for a set period of time. I love it because it helped me create a boundary around a phone curfew in the evenings which in turn, helped me to sleep better.

Asana

I first used this for work to help us all to keep track of recurring tasks so that we had a way to capture them and be reminded of them. Pretty soon after, I set up a new 'self-care project' and added in a self-care routine including some daily 'self-care anchors' to help me remain grounded, calm, present and self-cared for. Not only do you get a unicorn flying across the page when you mark a task as completed, but it's helped me to commit to my self-care practices more fully and regularly than before.

FreePrints

It occurred to me that I've documented Peggy's life with my phone and that my camera reel contains lots of precious memories and moments. In a bid to stop living in my phone, I've been printing off batches of photos each month and popping them into albums. We quite often now sit and look through these albums and talk Peggy through who people are, where we were and what we were doing. It gives her a sense of her history and us the chance to connect in a way that wouldn't have been the same if scrolling through the camera reel on our phones.

MyFlo
In the run-up to my monthly cycle, my emotions are all over the shop. I have a tendency to take things more personally, feel more tired and cranky, and to crave all the sweet things. MyFlo helps me to keep track of my flow so that I'm always conscious of where I am in my cycle. This helps me to tweak, pivot and adjust my self-care boundaries to honour the way I'm feeling.

Instagram
Of all the social media platforms, I find this to be the most positive – having deleted Facebook and Facebook Messenger completely from my phone. I've worked hard to make it that way though; I am mindful of what I want to be met with when I log on and have curated a feed that never fails to lift me up with content that relates, re-energises, and stretches my brain in the best possible way. Here are my top eighteen accounts to follow:

@mother_pukka
@poppyjamie
@chloebrotheridge
@mattzhaig
@allontheboard
@mapologyguides
@emmagannonuk
@ginamartin
@candicebraithwaite

@sophiehellyer
@ocasio2018
@harpreet.m.dayal
@seyiakiwowo
@lairdhamiltonsurf
@tombilyeu
@marieforleo
@busyphilipps
@jengotch

Acknowledgements

To write a book is a test of boundaries in itself; it's creating space, holding that space and asking for help from others to help you protect that space. Life decided to throw as many lemons at me as it could too (both personally and professionally) and I wouldn't ever have gotten here, to the end of this book, without the help, understanding and encouragement from so many people. I always find the acknowledgements the hardest to write as there's a sense that no matter the words I choose, I'm never doing justice to the people who mean so much to me or the feelings of gratitude and love I hold. I'll give it a good go, though.

All the thank yous to Domski for helping me to carve out the space to write, for listening to my ideas late into the night, challenging my inner troll, for your unending kindness, snacks, forehead kisses, love and consistent belief in me. Growing together and not apart is such a work in progress which requires determination, dedication and bundles of love, laughter and holding space. I'm so grateful that the future we work towards, and are committed to, is one where we're old and giggly and still holding hands. Thank you for being who you are and how you are.

Peggy, you are such a gift. You sprinkle magic through my days and being your mummy has been the most magical, mystery ride. Thank you for helping me to get this book written, by popping in with regular hugs, flowers you've picked from the garden, to make your funny troll face that you know will make me laugh and for making me so many handmade cards which surround my desk as I write. You're incredibly forgiving and accommodating of the fact Mummy needs to be holed away for periods of time. Thank you for teaching me so much – I've loved learning from you.

Thank you, Mother Hubbard, for everything – truly. I'm never going to succinctly be able to express the wonder, the love and the luck I feel in getting to be your daughter, so I'm not really going to try – I trust that you know it and feel it. Your WhatsApp messages of encouragement and your patience as plans kept shifting and changing with illness and life's lemons and things just not going to plan, helped more than you would have felt they did. Even when you're not physically nearby, you're always with me, in my heart and my head. Your steadfastness, rational Mum-isms, unwavering love and can-do-ness is like having my own personal coach and cheer squad with me at all times. It's because of you that I started writing again, thank you for reminding me that I could and never doubting that I would.

Ah, Clairie Wairie Airy Fairy on top of the Christmas tree, you don't half sprinkle my life with laughter. I don't think you realise what a treasure you are nor how much fun it's been growing up with you as my sister. Being a mum at the same time as you has made it all so much easier; the knowing nods, cheeky glances and suppressed giggles, as we navigate this mothering landscape together, has at times, kept me completely sane. There are memories I have of when we were younger that still make me laugh to this day and that's a tonic in itself. Thank you for all the times we've giggled like snorting hyenas but also for the love and loyalty, you're wonderful.

I don't think you realise how wise you've become, Dad, and

how you help me to understand some difficult, sometimes incomprehensible things when you give me an insight into how things have been for you. Thank you for opening up, lowering your Fort Knox boundaries and sharing your vulnerability with me.

To Auntie Ammy, Uncle Keithie, Wends and Adgie, you're all so loved, treasured and held oh-so-dear. From juggernauts, to poo-poos, all with such an abundance of love, the warmest of hugs and giggles. Thank you for being such a big part of my life and heart.

To the incredible Blurt team, you're all such diamonds. Truly. I pinch myself that I get to work with such passionate and empathetic people, every day. Thank you for your patience, your compassion and for being so brilliant.

I absolutely have to thank Amy Trevaskus, Tina Bernstein, Shivonne Graham, Brita Fernandez Schmidt and Rosie Johnson for being the people you absolutely want in your corner, cheering you on and I'm so utterly grateful that they're in mine as I'm in theirs.

I've got to thank Abbie again, in fact, endlessly. Without Abbie there wouldn't be this book, or any book. She popped into my life right when I needed her and sprinkled it with possibility and tireless pom-pom shaking. I'm so proud of you and can't wait to read your book!

Thank you to Olivia for hearing about this book and encouraging me to go full-throttle with it. Your nurturing nature was never taken for granted. I think you're magic.

Catherine, Amanda, Ru, Jo and Sally, thank you for nudging, reminding, flexing, tweaking and sharing this mystical world of writing with me.

To the hundreds of people who message me, and the Blurt team, to let us know that what we do makes a difference – a massive heartfelt thank you. Your messages have been torches in the darkness, slayed some tricky and sticky thoughts, and been like a warm comforting blanket.

blurt

BLURT EXISTS TO MAKE A DIFFERENCE TO ANYONE AFFECTED BY DEPRESSION

Being diagnosed can be overwhelming – there's a lot to learn and plenty of prejudice to battle. Telling people is tough, and not everyone will understand. That's why we're here for you, whenever you need us, for anything at all.

We'll help you to understand depression and what it means for you. We'll support you, listen to you and introduce you to people who've been where you are. We'll help you break down barriers and broach the subject with those closest to you. We'll help you help yourself, with a little knowing nod.

Find us online:

www.blurtitout.org
blurtitout
@blurtalerts
theblurtfoundation
blurtalerts

The Self-Care Project

How to let go of frazzle and make time for you

Everything you need to know about self-care: what it is, why it's important, why it's such a struggle and how to integrate it into day-to-day life

There's a damaging misconception in society that putting ourselves first is an act of selfishness. But self-care is not just a millennial buzzword; it is a tool that helps us to take responsibility for our own happiness – our physical, emotional, psychological and social needs.

The Self-Care Project is a no-nonsense, practical journey that will help you explore what self-care means for you, what your obstacles might be and how you can chisel out daily space for self-care in a practical, achievable and realistic way.

'Reading this is like a therapy session with a trusted, empathetic friend determined to help you turn things around, minus any irritating self-righteousness'
Independent

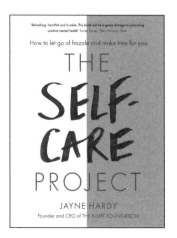

'Refreshing, heartfelt and humble. This book will be a game changer in promoting positive mental health' Sarah Turner, The Unmumsy Mum

How to let go of frazzle and make time for you

THE
SELF-
CARE
PROJECT

JAYNE HARDY
Founder and CEO of THE BLURT FOUNDATION

365 Days of Self-Care

A Journal

Everything you need to know about self-care: what it is, why it's important, why it's such a struggle and how to integrate it into day-to-day life

Self-care is a preventative action that focuses on our health and happiness, and yet so often it gets put aside when other things, and people, vie for our time and attention.

Following on from the hugely popular *The Self-Care Project*, Jayne Hardy, CEO and founder of The Blurt Foundation, helps us to plan for obstacles, devise contingency plans, be mindful of the way our days play out, and prioritise the things that are truly important to us. With the flexibility of choosing to start the journal anytime – on any day, in any year – this is the essential companion for bringing more self-care into your life.

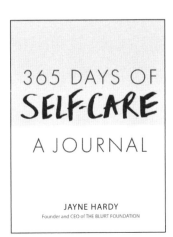